THE TWELVE STEPS
OF ALCOHOLICS ANONYMOUS

THE TWELVE STEPS

OF ALCOHOLICS ANONYMOUS

Interpreted by
the Hazelden Foundation

Harper/Hazelden

Library of Congress Cataloging-in-Publication Data

The Twelve Steps of Alcoholics Anonymous.

  Bibliography: p.
  1. Alcoholism—Treatment.   2. Alcoholics Anonymous.
3. Alcoholics—Rehabilitation.
I. Hazelden Foundation.
HV5278.T84   1987   362.2'9286   86-45834
ISBN 0-06-255444-1

87 88 89 90 91 MPC 10 9 8 7 6 5 4 3 2

Contents

INTRODUCTION

The year 1934 saw the birth of the Fellowship of Alcoholics Anonymous. A few years later A.A.'s founders, Bill Wilson and Dr. Bob Smith, wrote the Twelve Steps, which offer simple, straightforward guidance to men and women hoping to lead sober lives. Although the founders were careful to say that the Twelve Steps were only suggestions for living—not requirements for membership in A.A.—for over fifty years, these Steps have guided millions, helping them live lives of hope rather than lives of quiet desperation.

As guides to recovery, the Steps help us accept our powerlessness over alcohol and drugs. They stress the necessity for honesty about the past as well as the present. And they encourage us to embrace the concept of a Power greater than ourselves to handle the haunting stresses of daily living. When lived well, the Steps promise miraculous changes in our perspectives and our entire lives.

What you are about to read are interpretations of these Twelve Steps, written by men and women who have chosen to adopt them as principles to live by—men and women whose lives were far from manageable and serene before they were introduced to A.A. Hazelden has intentionally selected several voices to share their interpretations of the Steps, because a guiding principle of the Fellowship is that we should "take what fits and leave the rest." In other words, no individual speaks for a group or the organization as a whole. Each of us, in our search for spiritual, emotional, and mental helath, must decide for ourself how to apply the principles of *the program* in our lives. The application of a Step for one may differ, significantly on occasion, from an application that is meaningful to someone else.

The value of the Twelve Steps and their varied interpretations is borne out by the fact that over a hundred self-help groups, from Narcotics Anonymous to Overeaters Anonymous, have adapted these Steps and use them as their guiding principles. You will note that the authors of these interpretations sometimes refer to alcohol, other times to drugs, and sometimes both. At Hazelden we believe that recovering people must abstain from all mood-altering chemicals; all drugs, in fact, are equally harmful.

Because of the foresight of A.A.'s founders, there is flexibility in this program for living. This set of principles makes no demands on an individual but rather offers suggestions for behavior that will lead to an improved life with less emotional pain and greater spiritual well-being.

A careful reading of these interpretations will reveal that the underlying concepts are not unique. The founders of A.A. relied upon their own wisdom, bolstered by the collective wisdom of philosophers and cultures throughout the ages, to design the Twelve Steps for living one day at a time. You will quickly note that the philosophy inherent in the Steps is timeless; the wisdom is ageless; and, more importantly, the help promised to searching individuals is everlasting.

The Hazelden Foundation wishes you well on your road to recovery. We hope these interpretations bring clarity and purpose to your life.

Karen Elliott
Director
Hazelden Educational Materials

The Twelve Steps of Alcoholics Anonymous*

1. We admitted we were powerless over alcohol—that our lives had become unmanageable.
2. Came to believe that a Power greater than ourselves could restore us to sanity.
3. Made a decision to turn our will and our lives over to the care of God *as we understood Him*.
4. Made a searching and fearless moral inventory of ourselves.
5. Admitted to God, to ourselves, and to another human being, the exact nature of our wrongs.
6. Were entirely ready to have God remove all these defects of character.
7. Humbly asked Him to remove our shortcomings.
8. Made a list of all persons we had harmed, and became willing to make amends to them all.
9. Made direct amends to such people wherever possible, except when to do so would injure them or others.
10. Continued to take personal inventory and when we were wrong promptly admitted it.
11. Sought through prayer and meditation to improve our conscious contact with God *as we understood Him*, praying only for knowledge of His will for us and the power to carry that out.
12. Having had a spiritual awakening as the result of these steps, we tried to carry this message to alcoholics and to practice these principles in all our affairs.

---

* From *Alcoholics Anonymous*, 3d ed. (New York: World Services, 1976), 59–60. Reprinted here and throughout this work by permission from A.A. World Services, Inc.

STEP ONE:
The Foundation of Recovery

We admitted we were powerless over alcohol—that our lives had become unmanageable.

WILLIAM SPRINGBORN

The purpose of this essay is to stress that without an in-depth understanding and acceptance of Step One of the A.A. Program, a continuing recovery from alcoholism or chemical dependency probably will not succeed.

Despite some controversy over the use of terms, alcohol is a mood-altering drug or chemical, and, therefore, I use the words *alcoholism, alcoholic* and *chemical* or *drug dependency, dependent* interchangeably throughout this essay.

"We Admitted We Were Powerless over Alcohol"

This is the first part of Step One of the A.A. Program. It is very significant that the founders of the A.A. Program placed the emphasis on powerlessness over alcohol.

Many times we have observed people taking powerlessness for granted or with a casual attitude. *Understanding powerlessness* must be the foundation for any successful approach to recovery from chemical dependency, an illness that includes alcoholism.

Accepting powerlessness can be compared to laying the foundation of a building. A foundation has to be solid for the building to stand. A thorough understanding of our individual powerlessness must be solidly and firmly founded, or we will fail to arrest our addiction.

Some people we see in treatment have the attitude, "if I can discover the problem areas in my life, I'll be okay." For example, we often hear, "My only problem is my job; I'm not getting promoted fast enough; I can't get along with my boss," Or "My mate is too demanding, too critical; the family doesn't understand me." Some people blame a neighbor or the neighborhood. The most commom example we hear is, "All I have to do is understand myself (why I let things bother me), and my addiction will be controlled." With such attitudes, the alcoholic is failing to see the physical and psychological influences powerlessness has over addiction.

We cannot deny that there can be—and often is—a psychological as well as a physical dependency upon alcohol and other mood-altering chemicals. Psychological dependency is verified by the medical profession, and it is important to stress the psychological aspect of addiction. To be specific, as dependent people we have an "urge" to use our chemicals of choice. We all probably started using chemicals for many of the same reasons: to relax, to have fun, to be part of a group, to be accepted. But not one of us started using any type of chemicals with the express purpose of becoming addicted.

When we talk of the alcoholic's or chemically dependent person's "urge," we need to be aware that it can and does surpass all other urges. The urge to repeat the experience of becoming "high" is so strong that we will forsake many, if not all, of our responsibilities and values. We have thrown away things that are seemingly most important to us (such as our families, our jobs, our personal welfare, our respect and integrity) in order to satisfy the urge to become intoxicated or "high." We remember the good times we undoubtedly had during the early stages of our drinking, and the psychological urge to repeat those experiences arises. Once the urge exists, it becomes totally self-sufficient and will come to us in and of its own accord. We do not continually think of drinking or even drink every day, but the urge is always just below the surface. Even though we are not aware of it at the time, the urge to become intoxicated or "high" can occur at any time.

Reluctance to examine our powerlessness is as much a symptom of our illness as liver damage, withdrawal, or digestive disorder. We often tell ourselves and others, "But I don't *need* to drink or take drugs; I don't do it all the time." Social pressures centered around the myth that "willpower is all that is needed to control a drinking or drug problem" can result in unwillingness to study our powerlessness.

The social image of being a macho man or sophisticated woman is very demanding. It is not easy for people to admit powerlessness over anything, especially if they have not experienced social disapproval of uncontrolled drinking or drug use.

Negative attitudes are changing, however, with the gradual public acceptance of alcoholism as a disease. But the change is coming more slowly for the acceptance of some other chemically dependent people. For example, the "dope fiend" or "drug addict" is still considered by many in our society to be the lowest form of chemically dependent person. Many times, when talking with families of dependent people, we have heard, "Thank God it's only a drinking problem and not drug addiction." This kind of social attitude may interfere with people seeking the necessary help to control their addictions until a major crisis arises in their lives due to family discord, job difficulties, or loss of self-respect and self-worth.

Often the stress and strain of daily life, hangovers, family problems, job hassles, and other factors directly relate to the continued usage of our chemicals. This further demonstrates powerlessness in our lives. These symptoms are noted on the Jellinek Chart on Alcoholism and Recovery, which follows on page 4.

An honest look at these symptoms will help us understand powerlessness. It will also help us deal with the self-deceiving shadow of fear that surrounds our chemical use.

Understanding and accepting powerlessness is a way to freedom. We will be releasing ourselves from the insanity, the

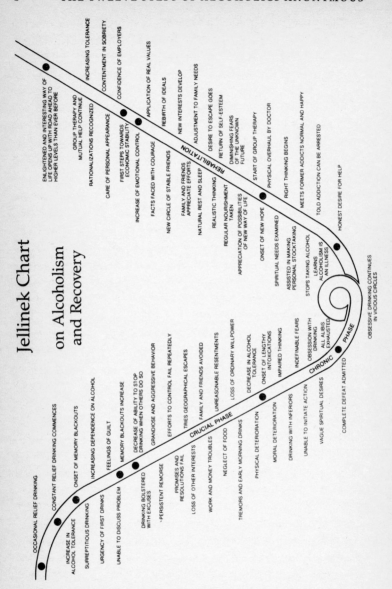

Jellinek Chart on Alcoholism and Recovery

Source: Adapted from E.M. Jellinek, *The Disease Concept of Alcoholism* (New Brunswick: Hillhouse Press, 1960).

morning shakes, the loss of respect, and the loss of interest in activities that have been important in our lives. We will be freed of the necessity to withstand the physical abuse of alcohol and chemicals on our nervous system. We will stop the deterioration of our liver and other vital organs. We will lose the faulty thinking (the deceit and lying that become so much a part of us that we begin to believe our own lies). We will become less subject to the moral deterioration and the loss of regard for our individual value systems. Ask yourself, "What am I really giving up?" You are really giving up misery, pain, discomfort, and a fight for mere existence in life.

Dependent people have an X-factor. This is physical powerlessness. The X-factor is so called because no one knows exactly what it is or why it exists. Many studies have been and are being made, but so far none has explained why some people become chemically dependent and others do not. We have even worked with families with twin brothers where one was addicted and the other was not.

It is important to know that we are *not responsible for the X-factor.* For some reason, our bodies initially respond to alcohol and other mood-altering chemicals with a superphysical effect. This effect is what allows us to develop the psychological dependency on mood-altering chemicals. Nonaddicted people may reach a level of intoxication, but the length of time that the "high" is maintained is much shorter than for those of us who eventually become dependent on chemicals. This may be the result of the X-factor. It is a fact of our existence! Similarly some of us have blue eyes and some of us have brown; some of us develop a heart condition or diabetes and some of us don't. Understanding the X-factor and powerlessness is essential in helping us overcome the moral implications and social stigma that imply that chemically dependent people are bad or wicked or weak-willed. It is such attitudes that we have to particularly overcome because they have been reinforced since we were very young.

As we continue in sobriety, we will begin to develop a program and a deeper understanding of how to live with chemical dependency when we understand it to be a disease we are not personally responsible for having. It is a progressive disease, and one that is more likely to destroy us than any other illness. If it is not arrested, it will destroy us totally as a person, not only physically and emotionally, but spiritually as well.

As we develop a thorough understanding of alcoholism and chemical dependency, we begin to understand our personal powerlessness over that disease. We are not ashamed to admit that we are powerless over it, just as we would be powerless over any other disease. We will also learn that we will not be able to adapt our lives to the disease of chemical dependency unless we have a thorough, ongoing program of recovery in the same way that a diabetic or heart patient has an ongoing program to keep the disease in check.

Personal responsibility for chemical dependency occurs when we have recognized it in ourselves, or others have pointed out the symptoms to us, and we realize we are afflicted with a disease. It then becomes our responsibility to start a recovery program. At this point, it is self-defeating to condemn ourselves for being alcoholic or chemically dependent.

We often reinforce self-condemning behavior with remorse and guilt for using chemicals. During the latter stages of our disease we experienced a loss of independence. We discovered that we were powerless over switching to alternatives instead of using chemicals. Just stopping the use of chemicals does not solve the problem. Physical withdrawal and fear of meeting life without our "crutch" have motivated us to stay drunk or under the influence of chemicals for extended periods of time. We have developed attitudes that continually keep us locked in rigid behavior patterns as a result.

It is imperative that we study to understand personal powerlessness. It is apparent to me from my own history and from working with people in this field that what helped us the most to identify powerlessness was taking an honest look at what drinking or using chemicals had done to us. Instead of living as free and natural people, we were reduced to fighting for survival in life.

The process of identifying powerlessness involves a certain amount of emotional pain, and dependent people seem to have a low threshold of tolerance for pain. Thus, it is so important that we have an atmosphere of care, concern, and reinforcement in A.A. and treatment programs. Dependent people seem to walk a tightrope in regard to the precariousness of their exact situation. We have to be made aware of the painful side of our alcohol and chemical usage and then be given emotional support as we work through it.

The need for the rest of *the program* is not diminished by stressing powerlessness. However, the significance of powerlessness in a personal recovery program is the essential foundation of recovery.

"That Our Lives Had Become Unmanageable"

Unmanageability is related to powerlessness. Many types of social pressures and stress prevent us from completely directing our own lives. There are two forms of unmanageability: social and personal.

Social unmanageability directly follows the act of taking alcohol or other mood-altering chemicals. There is little doubt that an intoxicated person driving an automobile down the street is unmanageable. Someone filled with amphetamines and pushing his or her body beyond the point of physical exhaustion is unmanageable. People under the influence of barbiturates or any other kind of drug will behave and react to life and others in a drug-affected way.

Unmanageability may be obvious in DWIs, arrests for disorderly conduct, or family arguments or fights after intoxication, but this behavior is not unique to chemically dependent people. Any person who consumed alcohol or other chemicals in the quantities that we have would act in an uncontrollable manner.

Often, such behavior can readily be pointed out in many persons' past. Think back to family gatherings or office parties: some have had "one too many" and have become more boisterous than they would normally be; perhaps they tell off-color stories or dance or relate to others of the opposite sex in a manner that is not usual. Such behavior definitely could be classified as unmanageability—and not only among chemically dependent people.

Our addiction directly affects every area of our lives. Our emotions and behavior become affected. In the area of our job, lost hours and shirked responsibilities are due to our usage of chemicals. Many people want to deny the total effect of their habit.

A fairly popular idea in our society is that alcohol and/or pills are the "demons" in our lives. I respect that view, but to a very limited degree. I am more inclined to stress the idea that it is we ourselves, not the pills or alcohol, who cause most of our problems. Chemicals will not bring destruction upon a person until that person learns how to justify continual use and abuse of those chemicals.

Personal unmanageability relates to the attitudes and beliefs that we have about ourselves, our environment, and the people we live with. In many cases, personal unmanageability was present many years before chemical addiction.

The A.A. philosophy is that putting the cork in the bottle is not enough. We need to rejuvenate our personalities. We have to learn about ourselves on an intimate level. We have to discover what the A.A. program calls our "character defects" and "shortcomings" to accept ourselves as human beings with strong and weak points just like everyone else. There are some character weaknesses that chemically dependent people do seem to have in common. One is self-centeredness. This defect has to be present in each of us for our disease to prosper. Selfishness seems to need a direct assault to break our denial system and rebuild trust in and concern for other people.

Another area of common personal unmanageability is the basic immaturity that seems to be prevalent among chemically dependent people. It causes us to respond to life in a self-defeating way. Immature behavior can also occur when we are sober.

Immaturity may not be obvious. A person may be able to function very well when sober, but the least amount of agitation or disruption of the normal pattern causes an extreme reaction. Overreacting is definitely immature. Any behavior that would result in diminishing self-respect or dignity is also immature. Some examples are temper tantrums, not sharing feelings and emotions honestly with others, insisting on having one's own way, and the like. Such behavior patterns enlarge and gradually take over a large part of one's personality.

Personal unmanageability covers a wide range of behavior patterns, because of the many variables within each person. We do have, however, basic common desires. We want to love and be loved. We want to feel worthwhile as people and in our everyday life. Fulfilling these desires can be much easier if we meet life on life's terms, instead of trying to battle and mold life into our own specifications.

The realization that life is bigger than any of us may be hard to accept at first. Acceptance of the First Step and all of its implications will help us learn to try different types of behavior, and it will lead to attitude and value changes that will allow us to become comfortable with ourselves and others. We must realize that we cannot control or manipulate the outcome of any situation, that we are responsible only for effort put forth.

I challenge everyone reading this essay to join me in the marvelous experience of becoming more aware of ourselves and our reactions to life, and to work toward the realization of our potential as persons. This can come naturally with continued work with the Twelve Steps of the A.A. Program, which is based on understanding and accepting powerlessness and unmanageability.

First Step Work Paper

The First Step is the foundation of recovery. The following work paper is designed to assist *you* in proving and accepting, on a gut level, *your* individual powerlessness and unmanageability.

POWERLESSNESS

A. How have chemicals placed your life or lives of others in jeopardy?

    1.

    2.

    3.

B. How have you lost self-respect due to your chemical usage?

    1.

    2.

    3.

C. What is it about your behavior that your spouse or family or friends object to most?

    1.

    2.

    3.

D. How have you tried to control your consumption of chemicals or alcohol?

    1.

    2.

    3.

E.   Give five examples of how powerlessness (loss of control) has revealed itself in your own personal experience.

    1.

    2.

    3.

    4.

    5.

F.   What type of physical abuse has happened to you or others as a result of your chemical usage?

    1.

    2.

    3.

G.   What is your current physical condition (heart, liver, etc.)?

H.   What's the difference between admitting something and accepting it?

Are you admitting or accepting?

Define how you are admitting or accepting through your behavior.

I.   What convinces you that you no longer can use alcohol or drugs safely?

J.   Are you an alcoholic or chemically dependent person?

UNMANAGEABILITY

A.   What does unmanageability mean to you?

B.   What could you identify as your "social" unmanage-ability?

1.

2.

3.

C.   Give six examples of your sober personal unmanageability.

1.

2.

3.

4.

5.

6.

D.   What goals have you set for your life?

1.

2.

3.

E.   Prior to treatment, how did you try to achieve these goals?

F. Give three examples of feelings you have tried to alter with the use of chemicals.

    1.

    2.

    3.

G. How did you try to change your image prior to treatment?

H. What crisis beside the one that got you into treatment now would have eventually happened?

I. What is different about you from other people?

    1.

    2.

    3.

    4.

J. Give fifteen reasons why you should continue on with *the program*.

1.

2.

3.

4.

5.

6.

7.

8.

9.

10.

11.

12.

13.

14.

15.

STEP TWO:
A Promise of Hope

Came to believe that a Power greater than ourselves could restore us to sanity.

JAMES G. JENSEN

What we have to say about Step Two is not directed solely to newcomers to *the program*. We do place emphasis on the needs of those who have just admitted to their powerlessness over alcohol and other drugs and to the unmanageability of their lives, of those who have only now recognized that they have hit bottom and who feel there's no place to turn. But, because there are no cures for alcoholism, only ongoing recovery, all of us, regardless of our length of sobriety, are working *the program* one day at a time. This makes every day a new beginning and each of us a perpetual beginner who can benefit from continually reexamining how we relate to the Steps. For those newly exposed to *the program*, we suggest that Step Two is not, in itself, a solution to our powerlessness and unmanageability. It is a simple statement made by recovering alcoholics who found the means of maintaining sobriety. It is their suggestion that we, too, can find sobriety if we follow their path.

As we look at Step Two, we must bear this in mind: *the program* does not issue orders; it merely *suggests* Twelve Steps to recovery. It would be unwise to automatically conclude, for instance, that the "Power greater than ourselves" is necessarily God. We have diverse religious backgrounds ranging from nonexistent to very strict. Even those of us who feel we have believed in God in the past may find that our relationship has gone awry and we have despaired of our belief.

We should also be on guard for any misinterpretation that the Step is an inference that we are crazy. Such conclusions can make Step Two a barrier to recovery rather than the promise of hope it is intended to be. But because these misconceptions can and do happen, let's define one way of looking at alcoholic or other drug-dependent "insanity" and then look at some considerations in our identification of a Power greater. We'll begin with the matter of insanity.

Insanity

The dictionary defines insanity as "inability to manage one's own affairs and perform one's social duties"—"without recognition of one's own illness." The first part of the definition certainly applies to those of us who have just admitted that our lives had become unmanageable. Assuming this is our first walk through the Steps, we have not as yet proceeded to the searching and fearless moral inventory of ourselves suggested in Step Four; thus, we probably do not recognize the full dimension of our illness. It is very likely that we're not looking beyond our drinking or drug abuse at this point and are still denying or minimizing the seriousness of the problem. We may still be blaming circumstances or other people for our drinking or using rather than accepting the responsibility for our own behavior.

It is also likely that we do not recognize the scope of our dependency. For example, many of us learned to depend on a variety of behaviors to help us cope with or run from the unpleasant realities of life long before we learned to depend on alcohol or other drugs for the same purpose. It is even possible that we have some very common and typical characteristics or personality traits relating to our dependency.

The late Dr. Harry Tiebout, who worked with alcoholics and was a strong supporter of A.A. for thirty years, defined us as "defiant individualists." The Big Book[1] identifies us as selfish and self-centered, driven by a hundred forms of fear, self-delusion, self-seeking, and self-pity. So, our illness is much more serious than we recognize it to be and, if not arrested, can be deadly. But it does not have to mean that we are candidates for psychiatric care.

Another aspect of our insanity is our distorted self-image. Somehow, each of us has come to think of our problem as being so unique that what will work for others will not work for us. These negative beliefs work against us and keep us sick. Take the example of a sick alcoholic lying in a hospital bed who has held all these negative beliefs. He's been drinking for years, very heavily in recent weeks, and eating just enough food to survive. After a period of intravenous feeding, he is now able to hold some food in his stomach and he's feeling better physically, but he's thoroughly confused and bewildered. He is filled with feelings of resentment and self-pity because he believes God created him in such a way that he can't drink like other men. He's also filled with feelings of self-condemnation for being such a moral weakling.

One day, two neat-appearing, quietly confident men enter his room. They tell him that they are recovering alcoholics who achieved their sobriety through a program called Alcoholics Anonymous. Our patient is immediately defensive and suspicious. After all, no one takes the time to make a hospital visit to a complete stranger, least of all a disreputable moral weakling like himself. However, as they continue to talk and tell him about their own alcoholic experiences, he believes that they apparently don't have any ulterior motives. But, he also believes that they could not have had *real* drinking problems and still appear as they do. He can't identify their self-respect and peace of mind for what they are; but whatever they've got, he knows he'd like to have it. Of course he feels that, for him, it's impossible. He is convinced his condition is different; it's unique; it's worse than any other. And while Alcoholics Anonymous may have worked for them, it can't work for him. It's impossible. And it is impossible as long as he believes he has to do it all by himself and on his own power.

Another example is the man who merely exists during the week, possibly not drinking at all or desperately controlling the urge, whose main preoccupation is what the weekend will bring. That is when he can really let go and drink as he pleases. Although he insists he's a social drinker, the nagging feeling persists that there is something not quite right about a man who enjoys life only when he's "under the influence." He resents his neighbors who soberly fulfill their husbandly and fatherly responsibilities, and he tries to tell himself that they don't know what they're missing—but he secretly envies them. Somehow, relaxation, enjoyment, and a feeling of well-being have come to be synonymous with alcohol. As long as he believes it is not possible for him to live without alcohol, he won't be able to. As long as he believes there is no greater source of power than his own, he won't be able to live without alcohol.

The female alcoholic has been called the hidden element of our chemically dependent society. Feelings of loneliness and boredom have overtaken her and her role in the family unit seems to have lost its meaning. She moves through her daily existence in varying degrees of sedation either from alcohol or tranquilizers, or very possibly a combination of both. While wallowing in self-pity and uselessness, she fails to see the full implications of her powerlessness and unmanageability and tries desperately to correct the situation on her own. She does this periodically by forcing herself to remain abstinent while she feverishly attempts to fulfill responsibilities at work or in the home that she has been neglecting. This may give her a temporary feeling of worthiness but, because she sees herself as her *only* power and control, the feeling does not last.

Consider all the varieties of alcoholic drinkers and dependent drug takers, male and female, young or old, who, lacking in a belief in a Power greater, have resigned themselves to spend the rest of their shortened lives depending on chemicals. Negative thoughts become so ingrained that they become reality—a distorted reality that becomes the barrier to recovery. This does not have to mean, however, that our sickness is of psychiatric dimensions. It means that in trying to become our own ultimate authority, we end up depending on alcohol and other drugs to support us. The true reality directs us to a source of Power outside ourselves.

Power Greater

Those of us brought up with a church affiliation or indoctrinated with certain beliefs may have a problem with Step Two, feeling there is a conflict between the doctrines we've been taught and what Step Two asks us to believe. We are not asked to forsake our previous teachings but, for the time being, to separate them from our basic need for a work-a-day program of living that focuses on our immediate need for sobriety. There will also be some of us who may say, "I already believe in God so I don't have to bother with Step Two." In this case, it might be well for us to ask ourselves, "Why, if we *really* believe in God, are we at this point of powerlessness and unmanageability?" Then there are those of us who identify ourselves as agnostic or atheist and immediately reject any suggestion that involves believing in God.

Step Two does not mean that we must immediately come to believe in God as He may be presented in some formal religious denomination. Because of this misinterpretation, many people dismiss *the program*, believing it won't work for them. In actuality, Step Two, like all of the Steps, is a suggestion made by recovering alcoholics that "this is how we did it."

They found that in the second step of their recovery they came to believe there was hope for them and that there is hope for us if we come to believe that the source of power we need in our recovery lies outside ourselves. They are also letting us know that this is not an easy step to take. As a matter of fact, it is so directly opposite to the self-centered, egotistical behavior we have adopted that it may seem impossible for us. Perhaps our task will be made a little easier if we do not get ahead of ourselves and keep in mind that Step Two is not requiring us to make a commitment. It merely suggests there is a source of power available to chemically dependent people by which they can be restored to the sanity that sober living provides.

If we were to ask all of the chemically dependent people who have been restored to sanity how they identify their Power greater, we would probably get a variety of answers. Some might say God as they understand Him, others could say God working through *the program,* and others would probably say that their Power greater was comprised of the Twelve Steps, the Big Book, and meeting attendance and fellowship. They would undoubtedly tell us that the most significant thing was the ability to step outside of themselves and to realize that they were not the center of the universe.

Coming to Believe

The actual demonstration that *the program* works for anyone who will follow its path should be our greatest impetus for coming to believe. If we have the desire to stop drinking and using, and if we are looking for restoration to sanity, we should find ourselves regularly at a weekly A.A. meeting. That's where the process of coming to believe is activated. When we are initially exposed to this process, we should not allow ourselves to be critical and judgmental, nor should we create unrealistic expectations. If we are looking for instant miracles, we are likely to be disappointed, for this is a lifelong process. We will see defects not in *the program* itself, but in the members, who acknowledge their imperfections. These are real people who are getting involved; these people are taking risks and speaking up at their meetings in spite of fear. They are expressing themselves honestly without regard for how others may receive what they have to say. These people are trying to be honest and genuine; they are getting reinforcement. These people are growing and maturing; they are thinking and acting rationally. And these people are staying chemically free!

They have come to believe that a Power greater than themselves could restore them to sanity, and so it has. What we have come to see is the evidence that *the program* works for those who believe in it. Step Two is not suggesting that we come to believe in any more than that.

Health care professionals and researchers may sometimes speculate on what makes *the program* work, whether it's the contents of the Steps themselves, the information contained in the Big Book, or the outlet provided in group therapy. But what really makes *the program* work is the witness of sober chemically dependent people and the foundation for belief it provides others looking for sobriety and the restoration to sanity.

STEP THREE:
Turning It Over

Made a decision to turn our will and our lives over to the care of God *as we understood Him*.

JAMES G. JENSEN

While Step Two can be considered a promise of hope, Step Three clearly calls for an act of faith. Coming to believe there is a means to recovery is one thing, but making a personal commitment to recovery is something else. We have seen it work for others, but will it work for us?

While Step Two suggests a "Power greater," Step Three narrows the definition to "God *as we understood Him*." It appears that we are faced with two very difficult propositions. One is to get out of the driver's seat and stop trying to be our own ultimate authority. The other is to decide we need God in our lives. This is a big risk—it takes an act of faith.

Many of us may feel we have little or no faith and may not even understand what faith is. Or we may feel that we've tried having faith in God before and it hasn't worked. Many of us may have no understanding of God at all or, if we do, it may be confused. Learning to have faith may seem impossible. But it is not impossible if we bear in mind that others have done it with success and that Step Three doesn't demand an immediate conversion experience. There is no time limit on developing faith, but Step Three does call for a decision. Short of a miracle blessing us with a sudden conversion experience, carrying out the decision to turn our wills and lives over is a daily, lifelong process. If we could accomplish a complete turnover at this point, the Twelve Steps could be reduced to Three Steps and ongoing involvement in *the program* would not be necessary.

In this essay, we discuss some of the implications of our decision to turn our wills and lives over to God. Because of the diversity of our varied religious experiences, we begin with some thoughts on understanding God.

God as We Understand Him

We have probably all known people who relentlessly try to defend their religious beliefs, or try to push their beliefs on others, or even try to prove that God exists. We may be turned off by such people and suspect that *the program* is offering more of the same. This is not true. Step Three simply assumes there is a God to understand and that we each have a God of our own understanding. Our understanding might be that He is weak or strong, conservative or liberal, out of date or even nonexistent. We should not allow our understanding of God to become a controversial issue at this stage of sobriety. We should simply accept the fact that if we remain abstinent and if we diligently pursue *the program,* significant changes will take place in us, including our understanding of God. We may find that as we learn to understand ourselves and other people better, we will also develop a better understanding of God.

For the time being, we should try to accept the definition suggested in the traditions of Alcoholics Anonymous: a loving God as He may express Himself in our group conscience. This will allow us to give proper consideration to make the decision and then carry it out.

Our Decision

The word "if" has been called the biggest word in the dictionary. It certainly appears to be a big word for those of us who are chemically dependent. *If* we weren't powerless over alcohol and other drugs, and *if* our lives had not become unmanageable, and *if* we were not prime examples of what the Big Book identifies as "self-will, run riot," none of *the program* would apply to us, including our all-important decision in Step Three. But we are powerless over alcohol and other drugs, our lives have become unmanageable, and we are willful people. And we are faced with some other big ifs.

Recall Step Two. *If* we come to believe, we will be restored to sanity. We can find sobriety *if* we sincerely desire it and make a decision to follow the path of those who have gained sobriety. *If* we try to be realistic, we will be less likely to become discouraged. For many of us, this will be a difficult time because our decision involves giving up alcohol or other drugs that have comprised an important part of our support.

We may not have freely chosen to go to A.A. or perhaps treatment. We may have been pressured by an employer, a spouse or other family members, a medical doctor, or even a court. We may not have a sincere desire to quit drinking or using and are proceeding with *the program* only because it appears to be better than the consequences of not complying. We weren't happy about admitting that we are powerless over alcohol and other drugs and that our lives had become unmanageable. We may have to admit grudgingly that *the program* does work, at least for other chemically dependent people. We may still be looking for a way to compromise—a means of continuing to drink or use drugs yet gain the fruits of sobriety, that is, respect for self and respect of others. But that's impossible. So now we must decide. Are we going to cooperate with life or run from it? This is the biggest decision we have to make.

All of us were initially blessed with at least a little faith, but we've seldom exercised it. Just as we must use our arms and legs if we want them to be strong and firm, we must exercise our faith if we want it to grow stronger and firmer. Until now, we have allowed fears of failure, of honest expression, and of rejection to govern and direct our lives. We must decide to act in spite of fear, not because of it. We are deciding to take some risks. We are deciding to act on faith. Turning our wills and our lives over to the care of God as we understand Him is the carrying out of our decision to act on faith.

Turning It Over

One of the intentions of this essay is to reinforce what the Big Book emphasizes, that A.A. is a program of action. *The program* works for those of us who are capable of being honest because we work *the program*. This philosophy, at least initially, may seem difficult to apply to Step Three. We are inclined to ask, "What do I do?" We may understand what it means to make a decision but we don't understand what we are actually to do. *The program* suggests that there's a great deal for us to do.

Each Step provides an opportunity for us to get to know ourselves a little better and to develop a greater awareness of where we've been and where we are now. Step Three is certainly no exception since the turning-over process requires us to be aware of what our past thinking and attitudes were and how we must change them in order to carry out our decision. When we do the Fourth Step inventory, it should greatly increase our awareness of what we were like before. When we are working Step Ten and continuing to take personal inventory, it becomes the means for determining what we are like today. It also becomes the perfect vehicle for measuring the degree of success we are having in surrendering our wills and our lives. There are many instances every day that provide us with the opportunity to test the sincerity of our surrender. We should ask ourselves the following:

- If we are faced with a situation that provides us with the option of being either selfish or unselfish, which option do we choose?
- Do we allow ourselves to be concerned about the needs and welfare of someone else or do we instinctively put our own needs first?
- Do we ever wonder whether our spouse or other family members are happy or sad, sick or well, or are we still preoccupied with ourselves?
- Are we taking the risk of expressing and presenting ourselves honestly or are we still trying to be people pleasers

in order to gain approval from other people—even at the expense of our own dignity and self-respect?

· Are we being tolerant of the shortcomings and mistakes of others or are we being judgmental and spending more time taking the inventory of others rather than our own?

· Are we exercising patience in our daily affairs or are we still childishly hanging on to the "want what I want when I want it" approach to life?

· Are we beginning to accept the responsibility for our own behavior and are we promptly admitting when we are wrong or are we continuing to alibi, justify, or blame others for our mistakes?

· Have we let go of our old resentments or are we still nursing them along, allowing them to feed on self-pity? Have we come to realize that harboring resentment hurts us more than anyone else and self-pity is only a step away from drinking or using?

· Are we dealing with current problems today or do we find ourselves still tending to manipulate or procrastinate without considering how our lack of action can affect others?

· Are we looking at ourselves and life situations realistically or are we still expecting more of ourselves and of life than we have a right to, thus risking disappointment, frustration, and a return to alcohol or other drugs?

And there's one other important factor to be considered in our attempt to move the focus of our lives from the material to the spiritual, and that factor is anonymity. The Twelfth Tradition of A.A. specifies: "Anonymity is the spiritual foundation of all our traditions, ever reminding us to place principles above personalities." We must diligently keep track of our motivation and regularly ask ourselves if we are using *the program* selfishly or dishonestly. Are we using anonymity as something to hide behind or do we see our anonymity as an opportunity to unselfishly help others without the expectations for personal recognition or reward?

These are just some of the criteria that can enable us to evaluate our progress in turning over our wills and our lives to the care of God as we understand Him. We can't expect perfection, but if we make a wholehearted effort and bear in mind the Big Book's admonition that half measures will avail us nothing, we should see continuous improvement.

Summary

Perhaps we could have been more religious in tone, making references to biblical passages referring to surrender such as "Thy will, not my will," but we have tried to keep in mind that A.A. was created for all alcoholics, regardless of religious background, and that the only prerequisite is a sincere desire to stop drinking.

We are convinced that for those of us who are chemically dependent, there is little likelihood of our ever arriving at an understanding of God, much less turning our wills and our lives over to Him, while we are existing either under the influence of alcohol or other drugs or are constantly preoccupied with our need for them. A practical application of *the program* to maintain total abstinence comes first. Then, as we gradually increase our self-understanding and ability to maintain sober and responsible lives, as we gradually increase our understanding of other people through a mutually supportive relationship with them, we will gradually arrive at a clearer understanding of God. This is what will continue to reinforce our decision and strengthen us through the turning over of our will and our lives.

STEP FOUR:
Knowing Yourself

Made a searching and fearless moral inventory of ourselves.

THE HAZELDEN FOUNDATION

Step Four, like each of the Steps, marks the beginning of a new way of life. It says that today I will begin to take a realistic assessment of myself. We hope this guide will help you begin to learn to know yourself.

Three attitudes are important: to be searching, to be fearless, and to be moral. Are you searching? Are you really digging into your own self-awareness and describing your behavior as it really is? Are you fearless? It takes courage to face yourself and what has really been going on in your life. Are you moral? Take a good look at the "good-bad" implications of your behavior. How does it size up with your own values?

Take a searching, fearless, and moral inventory, but don't be moralistic. You know your behavior has good and bad aspects. That is a fact of life. Look at it. Own your own behavior. But don't punish yourself. Our goal is to know ourselves and to accept ourselves. Only then can we begin to change and grow.

Give examples of your behavior that specifically describe your reality. Put this in writing, in black and white on paper, with specific searching and fearless examples.

Many have found it helpful to reserve a special section for facing things they have never shared before, the "what-bugs-me-most" behavior, what they least like to face in themselves, what they would find difficult to share with another person.

The Fourth Step is a simple and direct beginning to an

ongoing task of life, a direction to walk toward self-awareness, a way to go today and each day from now on. The moral inventory becomes a way of life based on the courage to be honest with ourselves.

You may experience some distress while writing the Fourth Step. This is normal. You may find yourself growing resentful, becoming depressed, feeling guilty, being afraid of failure. You may find yourself putting off the job until tomorrow! Share these thoughts and feelings with your counselor or chaplain and make what you discover about yourself part of your inventory.

This self-assessment may very well be the most courageous act of your life. If you need encouragement, support, and help, ask for it!

False Pride

By false pride we mean excessive pride—being so thin-skinned that we have trouble admitting any human weaknesses at all. Another word for this kind of pride is grandiosity. Describe how your pride has kept you from looking at your own behavior.

WRITE SPECIFIC EXAMPLES

Humility

Now that you are learning that it is safe to admit your powerlessness and unmanageability, do you find it easier just to be human? Being humble doesn't mean being weak. It means accepting ourselves—our strengths as well as our weaknesses. Do you know something now about what humility really means? Are you able to be less defensive, to enjoy the peace that comes with genuine humility? Explain.

WRITE SPECIFIC EXAMPLES

Perfectionism

Too often we are unwilling to accept human mistakes, our own or those of others. When we are afraid of criticism, we set unrealistic standards for ourselves, and we are frustrated if we can't meet them. When we're feeling this way, we are impatient with family members and friends and co-workers when they are imperfect too. How has your need to be perfect hurt you? How have you made others unhappy by insisting that they be perfect too?

WRITE SPECIFIC EXAMPLES

Admitting Mistakes

Most of us have not had much experience in admitting mistakes and admitting when we are wrong. We seem to give ourselves only two choices: being absolutely perfect or being totally worthless. What a relief it is when we can admit mistakes—admit we're human. Can you think of examples of your being in the wrong and admitting it? Is it okay to make mistakes?

WRITE SPECIFIC EXAMPLES

Being Phony

Being phony, conning, becomes part of our way of life when we are not being honest. We seem to have to look good to others, and being ourselves just doesn't seem to be enough sometimes. How have you been phony in the past? How are you being phony right now?

WRITE SPECIFIC EXAMPLES

Being Yourself

Today you're doing something important: you're being honest and responsible. At last you're just being yourself. Doesn't it feel good? Are you giving yourself enough credit for this? Are you giving yourself a pat on the back? How does your new feeling about yourself affect your relationships with others?

WRITE SPECIFIC EXAMPLES

Selfishness

"I want what I want when I want it." Think about that. Do you spend a lot of time worrying about your own needs? Maybe you don't get what you want. But what about all the energy you put into trying, one way or another, to please yourself, to get your own way? How have you hurt others by putting your own needs first?

WRITE SPECIFIC EXAMPLES

Sharing

When we're feeling good about ourselves, we begin to care about the welfare and happiness of others too. Have you learned how to hear other people, to see them, to know them? Do you know how to respond to the needs of others, to give of yourself? Have you learned how to share with others, to care about them? How does it feel?

WRITE SPECIFIC EXAMPLES

Impatience

When impatience gets the better of us, not only do we want what we want, but we want it right now. When we're feeling like this, and things don't work out the way they should and on just the timetable we set, our blood pressure rises and we can be really miserable. Describe some situations in which your impatience caused damage to you and to others. How does your impatience get in your way right now?

WRITE SPECIFIC EXAMPLES

Patience

Patience is an elusive goal: it's something we need to work on daily. Maybe we will never become truly patient people, but it is vital that we are not driven constantly by our impatience. As you work on your problems with perfectionism, do you find that you are more patient with yourself and with others? Are you learning how to take it easy?

WRITE SPECIFIC EXAMPLES

Self-Pity

Self-pity is hard to recognize, and it's something no one likes to admit. It's a matter of feeling sorry for ourselves. Maybe we feel people just don't understand us. Or maybe it's feeling that people don't respect us or don't love us enough. It means feeling hopeless, feeling like a victim of circumstances. Have you ever felt self-pity? Do you feel sorry for yourself right now?

WRITE SPECIFIC EXAMPLES

Feeling Good About Yourself

When we are working toward personal growth, we can begin to see the true meaning of "Love thy neighbor as thyself." It doesn't mean "more than" and it doesn't mean "less than." If we're able to respect ourselves, we are able to give love to others, and that's a basic part of feeling worthwhile. Are you able to see yourself as being worthwhile? Are you able to feel good about yourself? Try to illustrate this feeling with examples from your recent experience.

WRITE SPECIFIC EXAMPLES

Resentment

Resentful people hang on to angry feelings—angry feelings about our families, angry feelings about how we live and where and when. Hanging on to bad feelings can really make us miserable. Resentments are always good excuses for our irresponsible behavior. Talk about resentments you have right now. Do you hang on to angry feelings because you think your anger is justified?

WRITE SPECIFIC EXAMPLES

Forgiveness and Understanding

Learning how to accept situations we cannot change and how to understand those people we think have wronged us are marks of personal growth. What do you know about forgiveness and understanding? Has the ability to accept the things you cannot change become a part of your life now?

WRITE SPECIFIC EXAMPLES

Intolerance

Intolerance can grow from self-pity and resentment. Once we learn how, it becomes easy to blame others for the way we feel. Being intolerant is especially easy when others have different ways of thinking or living. However, it's also easy to be intolerant of those people who are close to us and who are important in our personal lives. How were you intolerant of others in the past? Think hard about this one: are you still intolerant of others?

WRITE SPECIFIC EXAMPLES

Tolerance

As you learn to accept responsibility for your own feelings, do you find that you are more tolerant? Are you more tolerant of yourself, more tolerant of others? Are you able to see the needs of others more clearly and to accept people as fellow human beings, to understand them? Are you able to accept yourself now?

WRITE SPECIFIC EXAMPLES

Alibis

How much have we invested in justifying our behavior to others by explaining for ourselves? Sometimes the explanations are true, sometimes they're partly true, often they're pure fiction. Can you think of ways you alibied for yourself? How did you feel about yourself when you did alibi? Do you catch yourself making up alibis now?

Being Honest

What do you think of yourself now that you're trying to be open and honest? Do you feel more comfortable? Is it easier to be with other people? Is it a relief not having to explain for yourself?

WRITE SPECIFIC EXAMPLES

Dishonest Thinking

Dishonest thinking happens when we begin making alibis to ourselves and believing them, when we really begin to believe our resentments, when we actually feel abused and misunderstood. The danger is that we will lose all contact with reality. How were you deceiving yourself in the past? How could you deceive yourself now about important matters in your life?

WRITE SPECIFIC EXAMPLES

Honest Thinking

Being honest with ourselves is the most difficult form of honesty. As we learn how to accept ourselves as we really are, we can begin to laugh at ourselves for sometimes trying to be something else. Are you able to laugh at yourself in this way now?

WRITE SPECIFIC EXAMPLES

Putting Things Off

Often we put things off until we get the right inspiration, until everything is just right. And the right time almost never comes. When pressure builds to get a job done, we tend to react by becoming difficult to get along with—by becoming impatient and irresponsible. List examples of projects you have put off while you have waited for just the right time. How did you feel when pressure built up to finish your work? How did you behave?

WRITE SPECIFIC EXAMPLES

Getting the Job Done

Have you learned how good it feels to complete a job not because someone is breathing down your neck about it, but because you want to finish it? How does it feel? Give some examples of things you have done recently that have helped you feel good about yourself. How do you feel about the job that you're doing right now of putting your life together again?

WRITE SPECIFIC EXAMPLES

Feelings of Guilt

Sometimes we hang on to bad feelings about ourselves in just the same way we hang on to our resentments against others. Feeling guilty can become an important part of our lifestyle, always there to give us another excuse for feeling miserable and behaving irresponsibly. Describe guilt feelings you still have. Is guilt still an important part of your life?

WRITE SPECIFIC EXAMPLES

Freedom from Guilt

Are you able now to let go of the guilt? Are you learning how important it is not to hate yourself, but to begin respecting yourself? Can you see that respect for yourself is really a basic part of personal growth?

WRITE SPECIFIC EXAMPLES

Fear

Sometimes we're afraid of specific things—afraid someone will reject us, afraid a plan won't succeed, afraid someone will find us out . . . and sometimes we're afraid in some vague, general way that we are bound to fail, that nothing will work out, that everything is going wrong. Talk about your own fears, the fears that you have right now, the fears that destroy your peace of mind.

WRITE SPECIFIC EXAMPLES

Acceptance

As acceptance of ourselves grows, so does our acceptance of the world around us. We don't have to be so fearful and defensive, because there's not so much to worry about. We know that we can only do our best and, after that, what will be will be. Are you learning to trust yourself and to trust others too? Do you find yourself being less afraid? Are you doing less manipulating?

WRITE SPECIFIC EXAMPLES

Taking Things for Granted

Many of us tend to take things for granted when things are going well with us. We sometimes forget the effort, the action, and the discipline that finally got things straightened out for us. Complacency or boredom are real dangers to our new ways of living. Can you recall instances when complacency or boredom caused you to slip back into irresponsible ways of behaving?

WRITE SPECIFIC EXAMPLES

Being Grateful

How do you feel about your new way of life? Do you show your gratitude to those who helped you build a new life? What are some ways you could express your gratitude right now? Can you see how feeling grateful can influence you in a positive way and help you avoid the pitfalls of complacency, boredom, and depression?

WRITE SPECIFIC EXAMPLES

A Plan for Living

Now that you have completed your Fourth Step Inventory, where are you now in terms of self-awareness and self-acceptance? What is your attitude toward change and growth? Are you committed to making some changes? How do you see Steps Four and Five now as part of a Twelve-Step Program?

To help you get at these important questions, we encourage you to begin making your own plan for living. As a suggestion, try listing some of your defects, the attitudes and behaviors that are causing you the most trouble, and make some plans to deal with these defects. List some of your assets and incorporate them into your plan for personal growth. Perhaps you have hit upon certain daily disciplines that are helpful. What about your new personal program of spirituality?

Write this material down. Try to be as specific in making your plan for living as you were in making your personal inventory. Then live it!

Step Five:
Reconciliation

Admitted to God, to ourselves, and to another human being, the exact nature of our wrongs.

EDWARD C. SELLNER

Some years ago, in my interaction with recovering alcoholics and the rehabilitation staff at the Hazelden Foundation in Minnesota, I learned that the Steps of Alcoholics Anonymous were leading people to a new way of life: to reconciliation with themselves, with others, and with God (as they understand their Higher Power). One of the key Steps in the recovery process is A.A.'s Fifth Step.

Baptized and raised a Roman Catholic, I had been to confession many times. However, it was only in applying the Fifth Step to myself and being given the courage to be totally honest with another that, for the first time, I experienced what A.A. literature calls a "spiritual awakening." Something significant happened in that encounter with a friend. In retrospect, I associate it with a turning point in my life: an experience of inner healing, an event that revealed to me a loving God who had always been so near and yet so far away.

Since that time, other people have spoken to me about their experiences with the Fifth Step. Some have described it in positive terms of forgiveness, new harmony, and release from feelings of guilt. Others have not had such positive experiences. Instead, their Fifth Step left them feeling dejected, disappointed, exhausted, and let down. To better understand this potentially important event of self-revelation, I would like to examine the Fifth Step closely and consider what contributes to making it a positive experience of reconciliation. Acknowledged in A.A. literature as one of the most difficult Steps to take (and one often avoided), the Fifth Step is also one of the most necessary to long-term sobriety and genuine peace of mind.

A Good Fifth Step Starts with the Fourth

Beginning with an admission of powerlessness in Step One and ending with a sharing of the A.A. message in Step Twelve, the Twelve Steps of A.A. have become, for many people, an opportunity for spiritual growth. Described by Bill W. as "steps backward" into the "universal heart" of humankind, they are seen as guides to spiritual *progress*—not to spiritual *perfection*. The goal of perfection or the characteristic of perfectionism is, after all, exactly what the chemically dependent person has to avoid.

All the Steps are part of a process that can lead to a spiritual awakening, defined by A.A. as a personality change or transformation, a new state of consciousness and being, the discovery that life does have meaning—in service and self-surrender. This entire process, of which the Fifth Step is a part, unfolds one Step at a time. Thus, when we consider what contributes to a positive experience of the Fifth Step, we must first look at the Fourth Step.

Step Four is concerned with a "searching and fearless moral inventory." According to A.A.'s Big Book and Twelve Steps and Twelve Traditions,[1] this step is an effort to discover the *truth* of our lives. Such a task is not easy; it demands honesty, thoroughness, and balance.

The first characteristic, honesty, is closely related to the courage to look without evasion or fear at our past—all the deception and lies, anger and resentments, pain and guilt that have accumulated over the years. This honest evaluation includes a search for personality flaws, which, together with chemical dependency, disrupt life and ruin relationships. Among the first things to look for in this inventory are resentments: those conscious or unconscious indignations and slights that can destroy people. (From resentments, A.A. writings say, come all forms of spiritual disease.) Those of us taking the Fourth Step for the first time will perhaps want to go as far back as early childhood to uncover resentful feelings and the persons and events associated with them.

Besides resentments, the Fourth Step should unearth areas that are now causing or have caused a great deal of grief, hurt, anger, frustration, or guilt. It should bring to light all those unresolved feelings, unhealed memories, and personal defects that have produced depression and loss of self-worth. Anything, any "secrets" that though perhaps "safely" hidden still continue to divide us within need to be acknowledged in this personal inventory. Honesty is of primary importance in this search. Without it, the Fifth Step will not only be worthless, it will be yet another harmful event of self-deception the chemically dependent person has already experienced so many times before.

The second characteristic of a good Fourth Step is thoroughness, a thoroughness that includes taking the time—if necessary *making the time*—to really examine ourselves (our identities can be discerned in our past). Anything worthwhile takes time, care, and patience, qualities often in short supply for the chemically dependent person. If the Fifth Step is to be well done, the Fourth cannot be rushed. We cannot expect it to be completed in a day.

Another factor to consider is the location of this self-examination. To go back over a lifetime, to thoroughly and honestly evaluate and discover what went wrong is a task that must be done quietly, in a place that has the atmosphere for such reflection. Once that place is found, A.A. in its wisdom advises people to write out on paper those things that have arisen in the course of self-evaluation. The writing itself often clarifies what really happened, what sort of people we have become, what needs to be accepted, acknowledged, and shared before it can be forgiven, healed, and reconciled.

In the actual writing, specific examples of behavior and feelings should always be included—not vague generalities that could apply to anyone. Thoroughness demands a willingness to get specific, to name concretely what happened, when and where it happened and with whom. At the same time, an overall pattern of estrangement might be revealed in these specific examples. Thoroughness, as necessary as it is, should not be equated with scrupulosity. Scrupulosity is another form of perfectionism—mistakenly thinking that every little detail of everything that has ever happened must be acknowledged. Often, a Fourth-Step guidebook (like the one that begins on page 28) can be of help in this regard, and we should never overlook the advice and experience of a sponsor or friend who has already participated in Step Five.

The third characteristic of a good Fourth Step is balance. Balance means not only focusing on our liabilities and defects, but also on our assets: the God-given strengths, talents, and gifts that we all possess. This means trying to find those things for which we are grateful, those gifts we can give to others. This search may be the most difficult task in preparing the Fourth Step since many recovering people are burdened with guilt, remorse, and a low sense of self-worth. Again, it is here that a friend or A.A. group can do the most to help us discover our positive attributes and begin to gain a more balanced, realistic perspective. It should be acknowledged, however, that often those of us suffering from a poor self-image or feelings of low self-esteem will only truly experience a greater degree of self-acceptance *after* completion of Step Five. Beforehand, claiming any assets or attributes may only be an intellectual exercise and not a conviction of both mind and heart.

For many who have been honest, thorough, and balanced, the writing of Step Four has been a totally new experience.

Although perhaps painful at times, it has led us to increased self-knowledge and even a great sense of relief. As one woman described it, the Fourth Step was a "revolutionary way" of self-discovery. She began to get a more realistic view of herself and her past without the self-delusions that blind all of us at times.

Choose a Friendly Listener

While in the process of preparing a Fourth Step, we should begin considering choosing a listener with whom to take the Fifth Step. According to A.A. writings, almost anyone will do: a clergyperson, a doctor, a psychologist, a family member who will not be adversely affected by our total honesty, a sponsor, a friend, or even a stranger. There are, however, certain attributes in a listener that will contribute to the likelihood of a positive Fifth Step experience.

First, the person being considered should have the ability to keep things in confidence. He or she should appreciate the highly confidential nature of what is revealed in the Fifth Step and not be likely to share the contents with anyone. Succinctly put, the Fifth Step listener should be "closemouthed."

Second, such a person should have an understanding of the Fifth Step itself. He or she should know the potential significance of the Step and the need for any chemically dependent person (and family member) to participate in it. In other words, the listener should be familiar with A.A.'s Twelve Steps, if not actually attempting to live them.

A third characteristic to look for in the listener is a degree of maturity and wisdom based on the personal experience of constructively dealing with chemical dependency or other serious problems. To be of any help in understanding and accepting what is disclosed in the Fifth Step, the listener should be able to understand and accept himself or herself. This includes a broad view of human nature and the ability to discern destructive and constructive patterns of behavior in others' lives.

Fourth, the potential listener should be willing to share personal examples from his or her life, since this sharing elicits greater confidence and self-disclosure. Every good Fifth Step is to some degree a dialogue, not a monologue. If the listener is unwilling to enter into a two-way relationship, the experience of reconciliation that the Fifth Step offers will be impeded.

The kind of person, then, that we need for a good Fifth Step is someone who can be trusted and who is respected yet is compassionate, someone who inspires more comfort than fear, someone who is to some degree a friend. Granted, a listener does not necessarily have to be a close friend but should have the reputation for being an accepting listener and a discerning guide.

A Fifth-Step listener with these attributes is not always readily available. Our task, if we want to have a good Fifth Step, is to look and ask around. Some of us may go to a clergyperson because we believe confidentiality will be guaranteed. If so, we should try to find someone from our own religious denomination. This allows for greater rapport. We should try to find a clergyperson who understands and appreciates A.A.'s program and the role of the Fifth Step within it.

Sometimes, in a residential or outpatient treatment center, there is no choice about our Fifth-Step listener. In that case, we should take some initiative in getting acquainted with the minister or listener *before* the Fifth Step takes place. That effort in itself can make the difference between a positive, open Fifth Step and one predominantly characterized by anxiety, defensiveness, and the inability to reveal all that needs to be said. Familiarity does not have to breed contempt; it can foster openness and trust. It is the unknown we fear; and, though A.A. literature states that a stranger may suffice for some, strangers are often mistrusted and thus not helpful to our experience of reconciliation.

With whomever we take the Fifth Step, we should keep in mind that we are not there to please the listener, but to heal ourselves. In self-disclosure, in being totally honest, perhaps for the first time, it is the inner self, the self that is trying to emerge in sobriety and maturity, that we must satisfy. Nor should we be afraid of shocking, surprising, or scandalizing the listener with the sharing of past deeds or specific incidents. The listener has probably heard such stories before or experienced them personally. (Psychologist Carl Rogers writes that what is often considered most personal is also most universal.) We should never think that we are the original "great sinner." This is an inverted form of pride that reality and the daily headlines constantly deny.

Step Five Is the Telling of a Story

After we have completed the Fourth-Step inventory and chosen a friendly listener, it is time to begin the Fifth Step itself. Step Four is primarily an attempt to discover the obstacles that have interfered with a happy and worthwhile life. Step Five is the opportunity, according to A.A. writings, for "casting out" those obstacles. Based on years of experience, the wisdom of A.A. states that it is not enough to merely admit to oneself what went wrong. In some mysterious way, it is only by speaking out, verbally acknowledging our mistakes, failures, and anxieties to another person that the power of those feelings and deeds loses their control over us. The past is eventually integrated and reconciled in this experience. It is only through sharing who we are that we come to know and finally begin to accept ourselves. All those actions for which we feel guilty or ashamed are like a psychic poison alienating us from a feeling of belonging, of being worthwhile, of being a part of community and of our own humanity. The Fifth Step is one major step away from a sense of isolation and loneliness; it is a step toward wholeness, happiness, and a real sense of gratitude.

How then do we begin? Quite simply, by telling a story, the story of our lives: a story that is often neither claimed nor accepted as our own; and often, because it's never fully told, it is never fully appreciated. It was in an event of storytelling when two men shared their life stories and openly and honestly acknowledged their weaknesses that Alcoholics Anonymous began in 1935. Storytelling has become an essential dynamic of A.A.'s ongoing existence. It is also in these terms that the Fifth Step itself is described: a person is to tell *all* of his or her story to another, all those things that stand in the way of inner and outer reconciliation with self, others, and God.

Thus, when we start Step Five, we should put the insights regarding our liabilities and assets that emerged in Step Four into the context of our life story. Rather than merely listing a series of incidents, for example, without referring to the broader context of our lives, we often find it easier to begin at the beginning with our childhood experiences and the relationships that affected us the most. It is there, with parents, brothers, and sisters, that we often discover the origin of many destructive patterns of behavior in later life as well as many unresolved feelings that need to be acknowledged. Somehow, by talking about our early years and proceeding from there, the Fifth Step is easier. Beginning at the beginning can also help the listener understand more clearly what is being said and perceive the overall character of our story.

In the context of this story, the important thing for each person is to tell *all* that needs to be told. If there is anything in the writing of the Fourth Step that we would consciously prefer not to share, *that* is precisely what needs to be acknowledged, either at the very beginning of Step Five or as the life story unfolds. Also, whatever has been written down in the Fourth Step is meant to clarify one's life before the Fifth Step itself. Those written notes can serve as a reminder of what needs to be covered in that Fifth Step, but they should not be the exact script. In other words, it is important not to adhere strictly to what we have written, but to let the story flow. In that context, too, the listener will probably find it easier to share aspects of his or her own story and thus enter into a mutual conversation that can bring about healing effects.

This practice of sharing our life story is recommended not only by A.A. but by psychologists too. The Swiss psychiatrist Carl Jung says that telling our story is the very beginning of healing therapy and that only by doing this will we be relieved of the terrible burden of guilt. Many people who have participated in the Fifth Step speak of their experience in these terms: relief from a heavy weight or sack or a sense of being cleansed. Whatever the terminology, many also have come to finally claim their stories gratefully as revealing a God who is forgiving, available, worthy of trust, a God found not so much in the distant past and in the stories of other people's lives as one discovered in the midst of their own suffering and, most mysteriously of all, in their own sense of failure.

We cannot change anything unless we come to know and accept it first. Nevertheless, very few people ever take the time to reflect on their life stories. They never really put their stories into any kind of perspective: the good times and bad, the significant events and persons of their lives, and the turning points. The Fifth Step is the opportunity to do so.

Step Five and Surrender

As much as the Fifth Step is related to storytelling, so also is it related to surrender—the act of "letting go and letting God." That simple slogan of A.A. is an implicit aspect of all Twelve Steps as well as the very foundation of the entire recovery process. It especially applies to us as we take the Fifth Step. We must surrender to the process of the Fifth Step by letting go of any compulsive need to control it or its outcome. We must also let go of any expectations we might have of it, even the desire that it be a truly transforming event in our lives.

This letting go is not easy since our expectations are frequently raised by others' positive experiences of the Fifth Step and by the writings of A.A. stressing its potential therapeutic value. Sometimes such expectations can lead to disappointment at the Fifth Step's conclusion because our own experience hasn't measured up; perhaps we haven't had the same tremendous sense of release and catharsis that others had. Whatever happens, when completing our Fifth Step we should let go and let God—surrender the past, turn it over to a compassionate God who, like the father in the story of the prodigal son, understands and forgives. A.A. says that spiritual awakenings are as diverse as those who experience them. We should serenely accept that Fifth-Step experiences will vary as well. The important thing is that we did the best we could and were as honest as we could be, not whether we had a tremendous feeling. There will be time for other moral inventories and other Fifth Steps.

The Fifth Step Is an Ongoing Event

The practice found in Step Four of making a personal inventory and in Step Five of "housecleaning" (as Bill W. called it) is not meant to be a once-in-a-lifetime event. Those initial Steps are meant to become a regular habit. Step Ten, for example, specifically recommends ongoing personal inventories and participation in other Fifth-Step experiences: annual or semiannual housecleanings that can contribute to ongoing recovery. They help guarantee that sobriety, health, and a greater degree of wholeness will continue. For this ongoing aspect of personal inventories and other Fifth Steps, two things in particular can be of help: the use of a sponsor or spiritual guide and the keeping of a daily journal.

The choice of a person to serve as a confidant or a "soul friend" is an ancient custom found in many cultures among people of many different religious beliefs. Such a valuable relationship, one in which both participants profit spiritually, facilitates greater consistency and a greater ability to get to know ourselves in depth. The person chosen should be dependable, trustworthy, hospitable, compassionate—all the qualities we naturally associate with a friend and those we sought initially in the choice of a Fifth-Step listener. He or she need not be a professional psychologist or an ordained clergyperson but must be someone who is, above all, a discerner of the heart, a person who understands and accepts others while in the process of learning to understand and forgive him- or herself. This soul friend, quite simply, should be someone who is attempting to live a simple pattern of life similar to what A.A. suggests.

The second aid, a personal journal or log, can be a way of making an inventory of our lives. We can record in it the events and persons that have had their effect; the areas of life where we feel angry, guilty, alienated, and resentful; the signs of positive growth, barriers transcended, and reasons to give thanks. Even dreams, which speak to us in the darkness of the night about aspects of ourselves that we would like concealed, can be recorded for later recall and reflection. Such a log or journal is not meant to be merely a calendar of events or a superficial diary, but a real effort to discern who we are and where we're going. This journal in all its honesty can be referred to when we're preparing the next Fifth Step; parts of it can even serve as a basis for discussion in the Fifth Step itself.

When we decide it is time to make another Fifth Step, we should recognize that we need not go back over our whole life, but rather take up where we left off when the last Fifth Step was made. What is past is past; what has been acknowledged once need not be discussed again unless certain incidents or feelings have recurred or a pattern of behavior we overlooked has recently been perceived. Whenever we take another Fifth Step, it can become an opportunity for increased self-knowledge, self-acceptance, and learning to forgive and seek forgiveness as a daily way of life. Such Steps also help us discover that there are reasons for gratitude, for celebrating—despite life's difficulties—the goodness and profound wisdom of God, the loving traces of His footprints in the story of our lives.

Conclusion

There is one thing lacking in any guide to the Fifth Step that no theoretical description can provide. It is the courage to proceed with the Fifth Step. For such courage, we can only make ourselves ready and pray for the power to carry it out—with the realization that if we do not take this vital Step, the process of spiritual awakening may not occur.

Whenever we are considering the Fifth Step and feeling hesitant about taking it, we should know that we're not alone. Many before us have felt the same hesitation. We share with them a common story.

It is difficult to live as we were meant to live. We learn slowly, step by faltering step, like a child learning to walk. We learn painfully in the school of suffering. One day, in our recognition of powerlessness, we learn surrender and what it means to pray, what it means, finally, to take the risk so that new life can be born.

STEPS SIX AND SEVEN:
The Forgotten Steps

Were entirely ready to have God remove all these defects of character. Humbly asked Him to remove our shortcomings.

JAMES BRANDON

Frequently, recovering chemical dependents say, "I'm still struggling with my character defects. I've tried so many ways to get rid of them, and they're still there. Something's not working. What am I doing wrong?" There seems to be a persistent feeling of uneasiness in spite of sincere efforts to work *the program*. These people have done careful Fourth and Fifth Steps but are still not finding the peace of mind that indicates serenity. They sense that something is missing, something isn't right, but they do not know what it is. Doubt creeps in, and the recovering person begins to feel inadequate and discouraged about the program of recovery suggested by Alcoholics Anonymous. This essay is written in the hope of helping people overcome the obstacles they face in working these Steps.

One of the potentially frightening aspects of working Steps Six and Seven is that they require us to deal directly with God. We are left alone to communicate directly with our God, to look at our relationship with Him in the privacy and loneliness of our own hearts and minds. Very frequently, this problem arises not because we do not want to work these Steps, but because we don't know how.

It is to be expected that these Steps will be especially formidable to anyone who has not yet accepted the presence of a Higher Power. Even those with a solid faith in their concept of

God and a strong religious upbringing sometimes have difficulty accepting the simplicity of these Steps. Early religious training may have taught us that we must be "good" if we expect good things from God. There is a feeling that we have to "measure up" before God, that we must "clean up our act" before we can go to Him in prayer. Maybe there is even a fear that if He knew us as we really are He couldn't possibly want us near Him.

Are we so ashamed of our acts that we cannot bear to look at them ourselves, much less share them with such a powerful Being? One must wonder if these feelings aren't present when we pray like this: "Dear God, I want to be more honest." "Dear God, I want to have more patience." "Dear God, I want to be a kinder person." We are praying for what we want to be or how we think we should be, instead of simply and honestly telling Him how it really is with us. Wouldn't it make sense, when we come to God with our defects of character, to make a statement of what our condition is rather than what we want it to be?

Looking Back to Step One

Let us think back to our struggles with Step One: "We admitted we were powerless over alcohol—that our lives had become unmanageable." Perhaps our prayers were something like this: "Dear God, make me a normal drinker." "Dear God, help me to control my drinking." "Lord, I don't want to drink like this. I want to drink like others." These prayers made sense to us because God should want us to drink decently, shouldn't He? We would cry, "Why can't You give me this? I pray to You, yet I wake up drunk! How can there be a God?" By now we know the answer to these prayers. Could it be that these were selfish prayers—prayers completely centered around our wants, our will for ourselves?

It wasn't until we could humbly and honestly come to Him and tell Him how it really was, until we could say to Him, "Dear

God, I am powerless and my life is unmanageable," that the healing could begin. Only when the struggle and fighting ceased and the acceptance began could the recovery process begin.

Coming back to Steps Six and Seven, perhaps we need to remember the problems we encountered with Step One. Maybe we need to begin our prayers with an honest statement of how it is! "Dear God, I am impatient." "Dear God, I am an intolerant person." "Dear God, I do lack faith." "Dear God, I am an unkind person." We need to present Him with the reality of ourselves, instead of our dreams and wishes of how we want to be.

It is not necessary to present ourselves to God in any other way than as we actually are. We do not need to "clean up our act." This is not what God intends for us. He is telling us that we cannot do anything to earn His love, no matter how much we give to church, how many good works we do, or how good a Samaritan we are. We cannot earn His love. His love is already ours through His grace alone. Grace is unmerited love and favor. It does not have to be earned or bargained for. It simply exists.

Whether we believe this or not depends on whether we have faith. What is faith? Simply believing in something that doesn't have to be proven. If a lack of faith is preventing us from living with some measure of peace, then it certainly qualifies as a defect—a defect that is standing in the way of recovery and our relationship with our God as we understand Him. Perhaps this lack of faith is the first character defect we can be honest with Him about.

Alcoholism or chemical dependency is described as a three-fold illness: physical, mental, and spiritual. Recovery has to take place in each of these three areas and faith in a Power greater than ourselves is a vital, necessary part of that recovery. It is also important to remember that even after we have found and nourished faith in a Higher Power we need to consciously cling to it on a daily basis. Even those with a long, solid history of sobriety and a strong faith sometimes waiver and need to ask for strength. Working and living Steps Six and Seven must be an ongoing process. Just as a plant has to be watered again and again if it is to live, so does faith. It needs care and attention to remain strong and healthy.

Maybe this is an area in which we could make use of the willpower that was so useless to us in our attempts to stop drinking or using on our own. Will is simply the power to choose. We have the power to choose to do whatever we need to do to nourish our faith, no matter how tenuous it may be. We can choose to go to meetings. We can choose to read the daily readings. We can choose to attempt to live the Twelve Steps honestly. We can choose to go to any length in pursuit of sobriety. We can choose to pray unselfishly.

So it is with our character defects. We can choose to identify them, to become aware of them and accept them, and, as a result, gain some measure of strength to manage them, instead of being managed by them. We can choose to share them honestly with our Higher Power, to tell it like it is and to ask His help in their removal, believing that He will remove them.

Looking Ahead to Step Eleven

A look ahead at Step Eleven might shed further light on our discussion of these Steps. Step Eleven suggests we improve our conscious contact with God as we understand Him, praying only for knowledge of His will for us. What is His will for us? So often we go to Him for help in making decisions: "Should I do this?" "Should I make this move?" "Should I take that job?" We want Him to help us make decisions, but we are really asking Him what His will is for us. It is my belief that His will for us is to be sober, able to face life with dignity and peace—to rely on His strength and guidance instead of alcohol and drugs.

Making such drastic changes in our way of coping with life requires that recovery be a spiritual process as well as a physical and mental one. This spiritual recovery is especially apparent when we look at the damage the illness caused in our relation-ships. Relationships with significant people in our lives gradu-ally deteriorate and are replaced by the relationship with our chemical of choice. There isn't room for those we care about. The same thing happens in our relationship with God, however we understand Him. There is a detachment from Him—a falling away. We think we no longer need Him. We have something else. We have a chemical that can produce a feeling of omnipotence.

An examination of intoxication reveals that it can be com-pared with a spiritual experience. When intoxicated, we experi-ence powerful feelings, feel a sense of well-being seldom felt otherwise. We feel powerful, able to do or be anything we want. We feel possessed of great intelligence and wit; we feel above the struggles of the rest of humanity. There is often a lighten-ing, a lifting of our spirits—a spiritual feeling. The thought occurs eventually, "I can make myself feel like this! I can remove the pain. I can give myself this wonderful feeling of well-being! Why do I need you, God? I can do all this for myself with the help of my chemical." And taking it even further we think of the fact that this miracle is right here—in this bottle or this pill! "I can see it, touch it, smell it, taste it, hold it in my hands. It has form and substance so I know it exists. I need no faith. So, who needs you God?" Alcohol becomes our god, a god we soon rely on and trust above everything and everyone, a god that eventually destroys us and those we love.

The spiritual healing begins when we realize this and turn to a Higher Power who will not betray our trust, a reliable God, a kind and loving God who can know us as we really are and still love and care for us. A God who can provide a sense of well-being that will not go away in a few hours. A God who can provide a sense of power that will not wear off. A God who will not take away our pain, but will give us the strength to carry on, if we let Him. A God who will guide our relationships with those we love. A God who will value our relationship with Him and stay with us always.

Steps Six and Seven

I believe that when we are ready to deal with Steps Six and Seven, we need to remind ourselves of our powerlessness, the same powerlessness we had to face in taking the First Step. We need to get out of the pattern of thinking that makes us feel that we are all-powerful, that our powers can remove these defects of character. This thinking is often the roadblock to successful completion of Steps Six and Seven. Just as we are powerless over alcohol or drugs, so we are powerless to remove our defects of character. We need help; we need to become ready to have God remove them. We cannot do it on our own any more than we could stop drinking or using on our own. We need to humbly ask Him to remove our shortcomings and then have faith that He can and will. All we have to do is ask.

The very simplicity of these Steps may be an obstacle to some. An overview of Steps One through Five may help us understand how this could be so. Step One, where we admitted we were powerless over alcohol or drugs and that our lives had become unmanageable, can be seen as a dethroning Step. Before Step One we were above, we were in the driver's seat and God, if He existed at all, was somewhere below. Step One turns this around for us. Step Two, where we "came to believe that a Power greater than ourselves could restore us to sanity," is a repositioning Step. It takes us off the pedestal and puts a Higher Power in our place. Step Three, where we made a decision, leaves that Higher Power on the pedestal and turns our will and life over. Steps Four and Five are action Steps requiring us to do something.

Then we come to Steps Six and Seven, and all we are asked to do is become entirely ready and humbly ask. After the tremendous amount of energy and effort we have put into the first five Steps, perhaps we just cannot slow down enough to realize how simple these Steps are. We cannot see that we have come to a resting place, a time for settling down. We flounder around, sure that we are not doing something we should be doing. We become ready and humbly ask, then immediately begin to wonder what we should be doing next. "What's the next move? How do I go about getting rid of these defects? How do I . . . ?"

What we need to realize is that we need do nothing more than the Steps ask. Becoming entirely ready and humbly asking Him is all we need to do. We can use this time for quiet contemplation, for allowing our developing closeness with our Higher Power to become a part of us—to internalize the knowledge and certainty that we are not alone anymore. Just as human relationships grow and blossom with honesty, so does our relationship with our Higher Power. With closeness to our Higher Power comes the peace we have sought for so long. This does not mean our troubles are over. Peace does not mean the end of conflict and pain. What we can count on, however, is the strength we will need to endure, to be able to face problems and say, "Yes, this hurts. Yes, I feel pain, but I know it will pass, and I will be able to extract some growth from this experience. I will be a better, stronger, wiser person for having experienced this. And with the help of my Higher Power, I know this will not destroy me."

Some of the problems we have living these Steps are self-induced. If a drowning person panics and fights her rescuer, she may die. If she fights long enough and hard enough, she surely will. Maybe what we need to do is stop struggling and let someone help us out of the deep water. Maybe we should let go and float, let the tide take us toward shore. Maybe that elusive peace is already around us but we cannot feel it because of the struggle.

The old well-worn slogans need to take on new meaning for us as we work these Steps, slogans such as:

Keep It Simple

Easy Does It

Let Go and Let God

STEP EIGHT:
Restoring Relationships

Made a list of all persons we had harmed, and became willing to make amends to them all.

PAT M.

Visualize this scenario: it is a hot September evening in 1969. A fortyish woman is standing in her kitchen. She is nose-to-nose with her seventeen-year-old daughter. The woman holds a smoldering cigarette in one hand, a cocktail glass in the other. She is berating her seventeen-year-old daughter. She is angry and scared because she has just become aware that her daughter has been using pot and has a boyfriend who uses it with her. The woman, in a loud and accusatory voice, says, "What do you think you will be like when you are forty?" The pretty, dark-haired girl looks through large, brown, tear-filled eyes. She responds in a cold, measured, and deliberate tone, "I don't know, but I sure hope I'm not like you."

1972. Three years later. The same woman, in the same kitchen. The telephone rings. It's her daughter. She's twenty now. She's calling just to talk, to share her impressions after both of them, each in her own place, have viewed a two-hour television show about alcoholism starring Dick Van Dyke. It's a long talk, and toward the end the daughter says, "You know, people are starting to tell me I'm a lot like you, and that really makes me feel good." And then—just before "goodbye"— "Isn't it great that we don't have to hurt each other anymore?"

1981. Nine years later. A postcard from Paris from her. On the front a fragile bunch of wildflowers and a verse:

> Je crois
> à la beauté de la vie,

à la dignité, à la bonté
je crois à l'honnêteté,
et je crois
en vous,
—MICHELE EMESSE

And, translated in hand-printed simplicity across the border of the card,

I believe in the beauty of life,
in its dignity and goodness;
I believe in honesty, and I believe in you.

On the back, "I hope this card gets to you when you are either on top of the world or when most in need of its sentiments. If you put it where you can see it when you're down . . . I love you and want you to know that you are in my thoughts a lot. Much of what you are is an inspiration to me, and I am grateful to God for such a mother as you. What sentimentality! And it isn't even Mother's Day. Please excuse my mush, but, sigh, it's all true!"

It is my hope that what I have tried to present here and in what follows will bring new life to the relationships of the people who seek it through *the program*. This is a short chronicle of reconciliation. It is the foundation of my own enthusiasm for the Twelve Steps of Alcoholics Anonymous.

The Three Rs of Recovery

Recovery. It begins with the First Step, with admission, at least, and often with acceptance and recognition of the reality of alcoholism or chemical dependency.

And the Second Step gives hope, through reconciliation, of the possibility of recovery. In Step Three, the changes begin to become more real and apparent as we set about doing the things that mean cooperation with *the program*. In partnership with a Power greater than ourselves, we begin a "searching and fearless" moral inventory of ourselves, and in Step Five we admit, as fully and as freely as we are able, the exact nature of our wrongs (usually to a sponsor, counselor, or clergyperson). If we have done a thorough and courageous assessment of ourselves, we will have usually done a "moral" inventory. Because it is moral, it will consider the effects of our behavior on others, with emphasis on the evaluation of such behavior in the light of our relationships with them.

It could almost be said that well-done Fourth and Fifth Steps start to "cause" the Sixth and Seventh Steps to happen. Why? Because for most of us the beginning of becoming willing and ready to overcome personal shortcomings and the humility to ask for help in doing so comes naturally after the experience of self-awareness from the Fourth and Fifth Steps. All of these first seven Steps could be called "personal" in that they are pretty much concerned with our awareness of ourselves and our personal, and often private, experience.

And a lot of people get stuck here for a while, self-absorbed, self-centered, self-conscious. Recovery can, and sometimes does, bog down.

Steps Eight and Nine would be the easiest for most of us to want to skip. It's definitely the "easier, softer" way in the short run to avoid facing up to making amends. Long-term satisfaction is far greater, however, as a result of having a "do it now" approach to Step Eight.

By the time we reach this point in recovery, most of us are becoming aware of how important it is for us to let go of the past with its painful, and perhaps some pleasurable, memories, to let go of hurts and humiliations, failures and outgrown successes, and to make a new life for ourselves, a life based on living one day at a time.

People are part of our past. And people will be part of our future. Relationships with people are what Steps Eight and Nine are all about—our relationships with other people and with ourselves and with the God of our understanding. A conscious and interested attempt to practice the first seven

Steps is a natural prelude to the willingness to practice Steps Eight and Nine. And that's important, because sobriety doesn't just "happen" when we stop using alcohol or drugs. And living with serenity doesn't just happen either; it takes specific action. In respect to our relationships with others, Steps Eight and Nine are the "how-to" Steps.

In this essay, I attempt to consider and define the ideas and actions suggested in Step Eight as they are presented to us in the context of the Twelve Steps of Alcoholics Anonymous. It is important that readers be aware that the interpretations and suggestions I give are personal experience and experiences shared with me by other recovering people and are not "official" A.A. theory. I would also like to emphasize what I believe to be the function of these particular Steps, Steps Eight and Nine, in the recovery process, that is, reconciliation and the restoration of relationships. Let's call it the three Rs of recovery.

Although these Steps are frequently lumped together by many in discussions of the Steps at A.A. meetings and in informal discussion among A.A. members, there's an excellent reason to consider them separately. Both Steps have to do with making amends. One requires thought. It is, in a sense, an inventory Step. The other is an action Step.

It makes good sense for most of us to allow time for the process of becoming willing, even though an Eighth-Step list can be made very early in our practice of the Steps. Willingness can have a beginning with the admission of the unmanageability in the First Step and there certainly will be a heightened awareness and more complete list after the Fourth and Fifth Steps.

Important to the en-*joy*-ment of sobriety is the ability to overcome guilt, shame, remorse, resentment, low self-worth, fear of other people. Changing, learning to live in harmony with ourselves and others requires the ability to let go of the past and feel good about ourselves, to become alive to the present, and to experience emotional freedom in the present. Reconciliation can be defined as "the act or process of harmonizing or making consistent things apparently opposed or inconsistent." The beginning of the act of reconciliation is the making of the Eighth-Step list. And so we . . .

Made a List

This is very simple. You could do it right now. Get a pencil and use the space below to write the names of a few people you feel uncomfortable with. Don't put why, or anything else, just a list of names. If you've recently done a Fourth Step, you've already written the "what," "where," "why," and so on. Now you're concentrating on the "who."

I made my first list as a very simple act of obedience to my sponsor. It took me almost eight months in *the program* to get around to it. That is what's called procrastination. As I remember, I only spent about twenty minutes on it, and there were about twenty-eight names. As I see it now, half of them, at least, probably didn't belong there. I realized that when I happened to find the list in my Big Book about three years later. It was then that I recognized the difference between real and unreal guilt and also a certain unmistakable display of grandiosity. I also noticed that the person I had harmed the most, myself, was missing from the list. I am glad to say that I have made considerable amends to myself and am still doing so.

I also felt some warmth and some gratitude when I looked at a few of the names on the list and realized that some truly miraculous changes had come about in my relationships with the people who were really important to me. It is sometimes difficult to recognize and describe the power of "willingness." The simple act of writing the names seemed to change me from a person who was thinking about the harm others had done to me (resentment) into a person who could own my own part of the pain in these relationships. I could actually begin to *feel* what being a grown up was like. I was accepting responsibility in a conscious and concrete way.

If you have made a written list, give yourself a gold star—now.

The act of making a list is really very simple indeed. Many people do not even try to work the Eighth Step, because they immediately begin to think ahead to Step Nine and they feel too fearful or guilty to do the Ninth Step. This is where the time element comes in. Just because the list is written, it is not yet necessary to make amends immediately, certainly not without a second look at the next important portion of the Step, which is . . .

Became Willing

Sometimes it seems unfair or not right to make amends when you feel that what you did was justified by something done to you. A lot of us think that way, especially in the beginning of our recovery when we are hurting.

The Big Book of Alcoholics Anonymous tells us that resentment is the number one offender, and it destroys more chemical dependents than anything else. Resentment is one of the many names of anger. Others are "carrying a grudge," pity (of self or others), or blaming. It means feeling anger now over something that happened in the past.

When we feel resentment toward another person, very strong and painful emotions are aroused in us in that person's presence and sometimes even at the thought of that person. In some cases if resentment is strong, we may need to retrace our steps a bit and rely on Steps Six and Seven to help us to become willing when the willingness to make amends is slow in coming about.

Resentment against another person binds us to that person emotionally and mentally. We are tied to the very person we feel we hate. The one person in the world whom we most dislike is the very one to whom we attach ourselves with a powerful hook.

The most effective means of overcoming resentment is forgiveness, of ourselves and of others. Forgiveness of others begins when we become aware of our own part in the difficulties in our relationships. Looking at ourselves helps us to become willing to release anger and condemnation of others. There is a phrase to think on here: "Forgive us our trespasses *as we forgive those who trespass against us.*" Forgiveness is a two-way street, and when we become willing to make amends to others, we do so first by becoming willing to forgive them. This relieves us of the bondage of old negative attitudes and gives us the freedom to relate to others comfortably, without defensiveness, phoniness, or suspicion.

All Persons We Had Harmed

Those who practice the first five Steps of *the program* in the organized and chronological manner associated with alcoholism treatment programs or under the guidance of a conscientious sponsor are usually aware of whom they have harmed by

the time they approach Step Eight. They are often aware that
they have harmed themselves at least as much as anyone else. In
fact, we usually find we've become our own worst enemies, and
our "resentment" against ourselves manifests itself in the form
of self-blame, guilt, and sometimes shame. Sometimes I hear
people coming into *the program* talk about their "inferiority
complex" or "lack of self-confidence." These are symptomatic of
a damaged personality, and much of the damage is self-in-
flicted. The serenity and self-respect that come with working the
Twelve Steps over time and experiencing ourselves as capable of
change is the best possible way of making amends to ourselves.

Usually our list begins with family members, friends, neighbors, and employers. Often too, it includes creditors, employees, customers, students, or others whose well-being may have
been affected by our behavior.

Some of us begin with enormously long lists based on a
somewhat unrealistic and exaggerated perception of the power
of our personal influence. On the other hand, total self-preoc-
cupation can blind us to the impact of our actions on other
people.

The length of the list is not the most important aspect of Step
Eight. Most important is to be as honest as we are able to be at the
time we are making it. At any point in time, our list is likely to be
imperfect or incomplete. It will include only what we are able to
recognize at that time. Growth in *the program* and the process of
recovery deepens understanding and increases willingness. A
new and revised Eighth-Step list is an option for any person at
any time in recovery. Step Eight is a preparation, preparation for
change in our relationships through honesty, humility, and
generosity.

It is very probable that you will hear, at some time or other,
someone who says, "All I want to do is stay sober, and if I want
to stay sober I have to keep my program simple. If I make it
complicated by making amends or any of that other stuff, I'll
probably get drunk." It is true that the primary purpose of the
A.A. Program is to help us stay sober, one day at a time. It is also

true, however, that drinking or using has a lot to do with how we think and how we feel and behave. If we are carrying guilt, anger, and resentment our sobriety rests on very shaky conditions. These problem feelings combined with fear create defensiveness and emotional insecurity, often the result of pride. The specific remedy for pride is an act of humility.

Humility is the ability to recognize and admit our limitations. It is also, for many, the beginning of serenity and peace of mind.

The Twelfth Step of our recovery program says, "Having had a spiritual awakening as the result of these steps . . . " The spiritual awakening most of us look for is often described by those who feel they have experienced it as a sense of wholeness, peace of mind, contentment, satisfaction, self-respect, and self-acceptance. We may never achieve this "spiritual awakening" if we settle for the "smorgasbord" approach to *the program*, picking only the Steps that "appeal" to us and avoiding Steps that, at first glance, seem to demand a courage we do not feel.

To be able to do a helpful Eighth Step we need to stop being "injustice collectors." Learning objectivity about the events and experiences of our past helps. To be blameless does not mean to be perfect. It means to be free from the need to blame—to blame either others or ourselves.

Making a list is also helpful in sorting out appropriate guilt from unhealthy guilt. It is appropriate to experience guilt when I have regrets about actions of my own that are in conflict with my personal values. Unhealthy guilt is when I judge my *self* to be bad or worthless because of my *behavior*. This kind of guilt is more accurately called shame.

As we become more tolerant and forgiving, less rigid and judgmental, we will begin to realize that "God is doing for us what we could not do for ourselves"; that is, we are beginning to experience real changes in our viewpoints, attitudes, and beliefs and are being made ready to become more active in the reconciliation process—and more ready to move on to Step Nine.

STEP NINE:
Making Amends

Made direct amends to such people wherever possible, except when to do so would injure them or others.

PAT M.

Before we begin our examination of Step Nine, a personal interpretation, I would like to tell you a little personal experience that has made me very aware of the value of patience in the matter of becoming willing. Reflecting on a particular relationship in my life, seeing "What we were like, what happened, and what we are like now," gives me a lot of faith in the power of this program. I'd like to pass it along in the hope that it will encourage others.

In the last two years of the active phase of my alcoholism, there was a widening rift between my oldest child and myself. Part of this was due to the natural process of separation she was experiencing because she was moving from late adolescence into early adulthood. But another part was hurt and anger, fear and intolerance on my part. I saw her, or so I thought then, making choices that I could not understand or approve of. And I was incapable of allowing her to live her own life without my input. Naturally, she avoided contact with me as much as possible. When we were together it was seldom pleasant for either of us, and the partings were almost always angry or painful. Early in my recovery I did feel the "willingness" to make amends to some extent, but I really didn't know how. To make matters worse, I could see her becoming increasingly involved in a relationship that I (armed with very little understanding or tolerance!) could only believe would bring her pain and suffering.

I knew that I needed to be patient with both of us. What happened was that the very relationship I would have deprived her of was the relationship that led her to Al-Anon. That was several years ago. Our relationship is now, I believe, mutually satisfying and respectful. We live by the same principles, and we grow in understanding as time goes on. God is doing for us what we could not do for ourselves.

Most people want to feel loving and lovable. Carrying a grudge or feeling guilty makes feeling loving and lovable impossible. We are unable to love, and we experience ourselves as being unloved or unworthy of love.

Many of us come into recovery with a lifetime of experience in loving and being loved "conditionally." Given this flaw of our humanness, we often experience the desire or impulse to just give up and throw away people from our past or avoid them whenever possible. Time in the practice of the Twelve Steps, however, has shown many of us that there is another option. That option is to come to terms with this "flaw" of ours, of loving ourselves conditionally. We can, for one thing, meet some of the conditions. I like myself better when I behave the way I think a "good" person behaves. And when I make an effort, I can become more accepting, forgiving, and less critical in my behavior toward other people. I no longer need to use my fault-finding skills to shore up my self-image by cutting others down to my own size or smaller! When I feel okay about myself, I don't need to check out my value by comparing myself with others. When I stopped drinking, I no longer needed to monitor the level in other people's glasses to be sure I wasn't drinking "too much or too fast." When I pray for help to be different from the person I used to be in a particular relationship, *it works!*

Honesty, willingness, and open-mindedness are needed to work these Steps. That means "becoming teachable," knowing you don't know all the answers and being willing to wait for new information before acting.

Often during discussions about the Ninth Step, one hears about individuals who make amends by making apologies. Apologies are certainly sometimes called for, but apologies are not amends. Amends are made by acting differently. I can apologize a hundred times for being late for work and this will not "mend" the tardiness. Appearing on the job at or before the starting time gives reality to my penitence. What I say about my behavior does not demonstrate change. It is my actions that do this. Step Nine is very definitely an action Step. If we took the liberty of picking and choosing from the Steps only the "easy" ones, I'm sure Step Nine would be the most likely choice for passing over. And so again, we need to remember that we are seeking the spiritual experience the founders of Alcoholics Anonymous tell us is essential to our recovery. We have to become willing and to take action, the action described in Step Nine.

John Powell, the author of the book *A Reason to Live, A Reason to Die*, has written something about spiritual awakening that seems to me to be directly related to Step Nine of *the program*. I would like to quote it here:

Somehow I feel sure that the most direct route to religious experience is to ask for the grace to give, to share, to console another, to bandage a hurting wound, to lift a fallen human spirit, to mend a quarrel, to search out a forgotten friend, to dismiss a suspicion and replace it with trust, to encourage someone who has lost faith, to let someone who feels helpless do a favor for me, to keep a promise, to bury an old grudge, to reduce my demands on others, to fight for a principle, to express gratitude, to overcome a fear, to appreciate the beauty of nature, to tell someone I love him, and then to tell him again.[1]

If we are convinced that becoming willing to make amends is necessary to recovery, we will also be willing to ask for help when we feel unwilling. Many of us prayed for help and expected immediate and visible results, without any consciousness of the need to cooperate with that help. How many have prayed for help to "not get drunk again" while in the very act of pouring a drink? Cooperation counts!

To make amends means to correct wrongs. Simply being sober is not enough. This point is well made in the Big Book story that tells us that "the alcoholic is like a tornado roaring its way through the lives of others," and it talks about the heartaches, ruined relationships, and uprooted affections that result. The story goes on to remind us how our selfish habits have kept our homes in turmoil. The situation is described as follows:

We think that a man is unthinking when he says that sobriety is enough. He's like the farmer who came up out of the cyclone cellar to find his home ruined. To his wife he remarked, "Don't see anything the matter here, Ma. Ain't it grand the wind stopped blowin'?"[2]

Of course the farmer's home had to be rebuilt, and we have to become willing to make an effort to reconstruct some of the damaged relationships that are largely the result of our own actions.

Some of us have been a little like that farmer. Being sober was supposed to be enough. Sobriety was a relief, and we did not, in the beginning, feel the pressure to mend our relationships. For a while that seemed true to me, but eventually it became obvious that I needed to do more. I imagine my recovery was a relief to some people, but this program was for *me,* and I still had some difficulties being comfortable around some people who had been affected by my behavior. I wanted to change that condition *for myself.*

I know a recovering alcoholic who remained sober and was an active and helpful person in working with other recovering alcoholics until he died of a sudden coronary at a fairly young age. I will call him, in the interest of anonymity, "Bob," because that was not his name. I heard him once tell a story about himself during a discussion of Step Nine.

He said, "There is one guy in this town I will never apologize to." Even as he spoke, he appeared to become tense, red-faced, and excited. He described a public quarrel between himself and the individual in question. (I'll call him "Charlie.") It seems that about eight years before during the latter days of Bob's drinking career, he and Charlie had exchanged angry words and blows at one of the three restaurants in the very small community where they both lived and worked.

Whatever happened, Bob, years later, was still mad. And so, every day at noontime, when he was ready to go out of his place of business to lunch, he very carefully peeked out his door to make sure Charlie wasn't out on the street. Then as he approached the first restaurant down the road, he tried to be invisible as he looked in the door to see if Charlie was there. If he was, Bob moved quickly on to the next eating emporium. And so every day, Monday through Friday, for one hour, Charlie controlled Bob's life.

Whenever I think about making amends I think of Bob, who was never able to "give Charlie the satisfaction." He was unable to make amends—for himself.

Before we consider the three specific suggestions presented in Step Nine, I would like to examine a little more explicitly three areas of amends: material, moral, and spiritual amends.

Material wrongs are wrongs done to others in the matter of material things: money, contracts, bills, loans, dishonest financial dealings, damages or injuries to people or their property, lack of productivity on the job, missing work or being late, extravagance or stinginess, money wasted trying to buy friendship or love, and money withheld to gratify self.

Moral wrongs include involving others in wrongdoing and giving bad examples to children or friends or to anyone who looked to us for guidance, support, or love. The area of moral wrongs can be very painful in respect to our close family relationships. Often we are so wrapped up in the need for self-defense and self-justification that we do become totally unaware of the needs of others, and we have done more harm in these relationships than we may ever know. Time and time again we hear of wives who have given up trying to manage homes and nurture children to supplement an income that doesn't stretch far enough after the drinking costs are paid; of husbands who take away the car keys and lock the liquor cabinet and whose work suffers from their preoccupation with worry and frustration over an unpredictable spouse; of children unable to enjoy their homes and ashamed to bring in their friends; and of very young children who feel compelled to play an adult role in the family because the parents act like children.

Often special occasions like Christmas or birthdays pass unnoticed or take the form of nightmares. Physical and sexual abuse, broken promises, verbal abuse, lack of trust—all of these may be part of moral harms. Childhood with an alcoholic parent can be a very damaging experience. It takes a long time and a great deal of patience, strength, and courage to regain the trust of an insecure child.

Spiritual wrongs is the area of "sins of omission" for most of us, the neglect of obligations to self, family, community, and God, the lack of gratitude toward others who have perhaps assumed our obligations in the matter of teaching or guiding our children when we made no effort to do it ourselves, the lack of self-development in the area of health, education, recreation, creativity, the lack of encouragement to others in our lives. The beginning of sobriety is often accompanied by the new aware-ness and appreciation of the fact that, in spite of our self-destructive behavior, we are alive and we do have a chance to change by accepting help and by living *the program*, one day at a time.

So let's now go over the three important suggestions made in Step Nine.

"Made Direct Amends to Such People"

The important word here is "direct." Being indirect in making amends is not as effective in bringing about the behavior and character change that leads to maturity. We might want to be indirect because it seems easier. For example, it might seem easier just to pay an old debt anonymously by mail. Justice might be done this way, but Step Nine is to help us gain humility, honesty, and courage, and that means we need to go directly to the people we have harmed, make direct restitution, and directly admit our wrongs. Directness serves a purpose beyond justice. It summons honesty and courage to our service and gives us the freedom to look others in the eye and experience self-respect equal to the respect we sense in others.

In most cases direct amends are received well, and even in those rare cases where they are not, this is not a reason to avoid the effort next time. If people are unable to accept a sincere offer of restitution, then perhaps their part of the problem will have to remain unresolved. This is a good place to use the Serenity Prayer.[3] It is helpful to remember that our expectations about "results" can get in the way of our own ability to accept the outcome. A prayerful approach and a willingness to do God's will help us to recognize our own humanness and encourage realistic expectations of other humans.

In most cases, relationships improve markedly when amends are made.

"Wherever Possible"

There are, of course, some cases where direct amends are not possible. This may be because there are people who are no longer part of our lives, either because we have lost contact with them completely or because they have died. In these cases an indirect amend can often satisfy our need to "make things right." If the harm has been a money matter, it can often be remedied by paying a debt to a survivor or by making a contribution to a charitable cause in that person's name. We can also make indirect amends through prayer. People in *the program* have told me of their practice of making amends through doing a kindness for someone else's child or parent when they no longer had any possibility of caring for their own. I cannot relive the years of my children's childhood and adolescence and thereby undo all my wrongs and mistakes. And it is not appropriate, now that my children are adults, to give them what they needed at age five or fifteen. However, I can sometimes share strength with another child whose parent is unable or even help the disabled parent in some way. The point is, I must pray for guidance about these amends and see the opportunities when they are there. The best way I can make amends to my now-adult children is to respect them as adults while I maintain my own recovery and be a healthy and reasonably happy adult myself.

It is important to remember, in respect to this Step in particular, that even though we may begin relatively soon to work on it, it is, like all of the Steps, a lifetime proposition. Recovery is a process that takes a lifetime. Step Nine is an action Step, but the action has to be tempered by common sense, and some of us need time to develop that. It's not helpful to go rushing off in all directions trying to immediately remedy all the harm we've done in our lifetime. We need to grow personally and to develop wisdom, good judgment, and the willingness to forgive and be forgiven.

Of course, neither should we avoid making amends by ignoring appropriate opportunities. If we are truly willing, and if we ask and look for guidance, the opportunities will come, perhaps not on our time schedule, but by the grace of God, when we are spiritually developed enough to use them constructively.

"Except When To Do So Would Injure Them Or Others"

Knowing when making amends would injure is tricky. One situation that comes up rather often is the case of marital infidelity. Making amends here may indeed involve harm to others and can also be a very selfish way of unloading guilt over the past at the expense of someone else's reputation or peace of mind.

In cases like this, simply changing behavior without documenting past sins to the victim is sometimes the kindest way to do the job. Sometimes I have myself had the experience of having someone trying to make amends to me and I have wanted to say, "Don't explain. Just change!" Who really needs to know why? I think when I was new in *the program*, I became, for a while at least, a "habitual explainer." How boring!

Another example is the parent who, overcome with guilt about neglect or abuse of a child in the past, becomes overprotective or overindulgent toward children who may be long past the age when parents ought to be protective and provident. It really is more appropriate to support and encourage self-reliance and independence in later childhood. Each situation is unique. You have been given examples of some guidelines. There is sound advice about general principles in the A.A. literature. A.A. groups and, in particular, A.A. sponsors can be of help in a doubtful situation.

A strong sponsor is a great asset in helping us to become aware and honest about our own motives in making amends. It might be easy to fall back on the phrase "except when to do so . . . " if we are looking for a way out because of possible inconvenience or undesirable consequences to ourselves or if we are using "making amends" as a way of meeting our own needs at the expense of another person's peace of mind. Motivation has to be examined in the light of honesty, and most of us do better when we share our thoughts with a sponsor before acting in uncertain situations.

Steps Eight and Nine allow us to make amends to ourselves by rebuilding self-esteem. Many people think of them as a way of "doing penance" or paying debts. They are. But they are more. Atonement, *at-one-ment,* is to feel in good standing with ourselves and others. This means that the payoff for these Steps is a gradual but increasingly rewarding sense of self-acceptance and self-respect, being in harmony with our own personal world.

The side effects of making amends to self are finding a better way to live and a better way to love. These are the Steps of reconciliation, and they are the Steps that bring us back into good relationships with other people.

The greatest spiritual failure of the active drinker or user is the failure to love and the failure to appreciate; this is the basic task involved in making amends to God, the task of learning how to love, to rid ourselves of resentment and resistance, and to become open to other people. Anything that comes between us and other people cuts us off from the Power greater than ourselves of Step Two.

Most of us need to ask for help, to have the honesty, courage, and humility to take action in making amends. The best way I know to ask for what is needed to work Steps Eight and Nine is expressed completely in the prayer known as "The Prayer of St. Francis." The prayer says:

Lord, make me an instrument of your peace
  Where there is hatred, let me sow love
  Where there is injury, pardon
  Where there is doubt, faith
  Where there is despair, hope
  Where there is darkness, light
  Where there is sadness, joy.
O Divine Master, grant that I may not so much seek
  To be consoled, as to console
  To be understood, as to understand
  To be loved, as to love.
For
  It is in giving that we receive
  It is in pardoning that we are pardoned
  It is in dying that we are born to eternal life.

STEP TEN:
A Good Tenth Step

Continued to take personal inventory and when we
were wrong promptly admitted it.

MEL B.

The price of freedom, it's often said, is eternal vigilance.

As a recovering alcoholic, I tie that old saying to the Tenth
Step of the Alcoholics Anonymous Program: "Continued to
take personal inventory and when we were wrong promptly
admitted it." Lasting freedom from alcohol or drugs has its
price, and so does the happiness we want in sobriety. That price
is eternal vigilance in taking inventory.

Most people acknowledge that the Tenth Step is a good
guideline *for the other person.* We often wish others would admit
their wrongs more promptly than they do. But what's hard to
see is that *we* need to take inventory even when we are doing
well. In sobriety, recovering chemical dependents can appear
terribly moral simply because they've stopped fighting cops
and passing no-fund checks. It's easy to ask, "Why should I
continue to take inventory now that I've rejoined the human
race and am behaving about as well as the nonalcoholics who
used to criticize me?"

Well, we might be fortunate that the author of the Twelve
Steps was a stockbroker and borrowed lessons from the world
of business. "A business that takes no regular inventory usually goes broke," Bill W. wrote. "Taking a commercial inventory
is a fact-finding and a fact-facing process. . . . One object is to
disclose damaged or unsaleable goods, to get rid of them

promptly and without regret. If the owner of a business is to be successful, he cannot fool himself about values."[1]

I knew something about that. Back in the Depression, my father conducted a bankruptcy sale for a merchant whose inventory included items dating back to World War I. I particularly remember hundreds of pairs of women's high button shoes that were at least twenty years out of date. The store owner had not been able to admit that he had worthless items in stock. This weakness destroyed his business. And on the positive side, I was impressed by the memoirs of a famous speculator who had made millions in the stock market. He said that his success was partly due to his readiness to admit a mistake when he had made a bad buy. He would sell the bad stocks before prices fell even lower, thereby cutting his losses.

Those lessons apply with great force in the lives of recovering alcoholics and other chemical dependents. In the business of living sober, we can't afford to hang on to useless, harmful attitudes and practices. If we're making mistakes or seem to be on a wrong course in any department of our lives, the sooner we admit it, the better chance we have of cutting our losses, that is, reducing the pain and harm we may be causing. We do that by working the Tenth Step.

The Tenth Step is actually a daily visit with Steps Four through Nine of the A.A. Program. These "inventory and restitution" Steps are the great housecleaning that is suggested for a chemical dependent's recovery. In writing about this housecleaning process, our friend Bill W. called it something that should continue for a lifetime. "Continue to watch for selfishness, dishonesty, resentment, and fear," he wrote. "When these crop up, we ask God at once to remove them. We discuss them with someone immediately and make amends quickly if we have harmed anyone."[2]

Three Areas to Watch

In A.A., we hear a lot about selfishness, dishonesty, resentment, and fear. I find them appearing at several levels in my life.

The three areas that require constant scrutiny are: thoughts and motives, words, and actions. All of them can get me into trouble.

I've learned to look at my thoughts and motives first, because most of my mistakes start there. "A man is literally *what he thinks*," James Allen writes, "his character being the complete sum of all his thoughts."[3] I can't argue with that, because too many A.A. members have warned us to watch out for "stinking thinking." If I watch the way I think and feel, the words and actions usually turn out all right.

But what a job it is to keep one's thinking straight! Time and again, my daily inventory has turned up bad motives behind actions that seemed okay on the surface. One day, for example, I was embarrassed to discover that the people I usually talked with at A.A. meetings were attractive women, successful business and professional people, or individuals whose backgrounds and personalities interested me. I had really been meeting my own needs for self-esteem and companionship when I thought I was carrying the A.A. message. Another time I met a destitute man in our company parking lot and drove him to a place where he could obtain medicine. But while performing this act of seeming kindness, I was smugly telling myself that none of the other management people in the company would have bothered to help this person. So I was playing the role of good Samaritan to feel superior to others whom I sometimes feared and resented.

The daily inventory also turns up garbage from the past, or what I now call "old tapes." Sometimes I discover that I'm still trying to prove myself to people who disapproved of me. Now and then, a minor incident causes considerable pain and I realize that it reminds me of a past defeat or humiliation I haven't yet released. A few years after getting sober, I went to visit family members who remembered me as a drunken ne'er-do-well. I packed two unneeded suits for the trip just to prove I was no longer a bum!

Another problem that daily inventory revealed was a tendency to "righteous anger." I could lose my temper and then immediately blame this on some fault in the other person. As I saw it, I had a right to become angry because the other person was behaving so badly. Yet, something had to be wrong with this anger because it left a feeling of depression and guilt. One day, it helped when an A.A. speaker pointed out that we are letting other people control our moods if we let them "make us angry." It helped even more when I realized that my anger wasn't necessarily related to what other people said or did. It really grew out of my own fears, anxieties, and feelings of insecurity.

It is much more comfortable to deal with thoughts and feelings before they are expressed. There have been times, even recently, when my anger has gone out of control and caused me to say or do things I regretted almost immediately. There is only one right way to handle such lapses and that is to admit the wrong immediately and make direct amends if necessary. Sometimes this requires me to make amends to people who have been rather nasty toward me. But that should be no concern of mine, although it takes some pocketing of pride to get the job done. People who find themselves in this position should remember that the recovering chemical dependent's primary goal is to stay sober and find self-improvement in *the program*. If amends should be made to strengthen sobriety and character, it's always best to push pride aside and do the right and necessary thing.

Three Kinds of Camouflages

Pride has a way of playing other tricks on us in the inventory process. One way of avoiding inventory is by disguising or camouflaging our wrongs. This can be done with the Drunkalog, the Blanket Admission, or the Partial Admission. Each can be harmful in its own way.

The Drunkalog, a person's drinking story, presents a special danger because of the emphasis A.A. places on "qualifying" as an alcoholic and sharing one's experience. We should not discredit or eliminate personal accounts of drinking experience. These testimonies convince newcomers that we are like them and can understand their problems. The process of "one alcoholic talking to another" still carries a big wallop.

The principal shortcoming of the Drunkalog, however, is that it is about the *past*. A powerful speaker can electrify an A.A. audience with a gripping tale or horrors from a drunken past. If the story is good enough, neither the speaker nor listeners will even bother to ask how things are shaping up *today*. The truth could be that a refusal to take continuous inventory is causing havoc *here and now*. In some ways, it's really more important to focus on minor problems today than on the major shortcomings of the past, even if the current problems are less interesting.

A second camouflage for inventory taking is the Blanket Admission. In this, the person makes a complete and total confession of wrong. One often hears, "When I came into A.A., I was bankrupt in every respect. I was a louse in all departments of my life. Nothing was right." At first glance, this statement seems to express great honesty and courage. In some cases, it does. But it can also be a lazy or fearful person's way of avoiding the hard questions about life and behavior. It can be a way of hiding specific matters that are disturbing and frightening. The Blanket Admission can be a barrier to a searching and fearless moral inventory at the beginning of one's A.A. experience, and it also can block further inventories later on. It is neither a fact-finding nor a fact-facing process.

Still another barrier to inventory is the Partial Admission, which also could be called "inventory with self-justification." I have been rather good at using this camouflage. It's done by admitting my own wrong or error, and then immediately going on to point out that another person also is at fault in the matter. Without too much effort, I could start out by accepting the blame and then transfer most of it to the other person by the time I'd finished. I frequently used the Partial Admission when I apologized for blowing up at one of my children."I'm sorry I bawled you out," I would say, "but I'm sick and tired of the way you leave your things laying around!" I also worked in an office where we gossiped endlessly and destructively about the boss. Sometimes I would admit that the gossip was wrong, and then quickly add that the boss deserved it or had brought it on himself.

There might be other ways to camouflage our wrongs. All we need to know about the subject, however, is that human pride and fear are always working to keep us from the painful task of dealing with our own faults. Bad thinking, like alcohol or drugs, is cunning, baffling, and powerful!

When Are We Wrong?

One of my most useful discoveries has been that wrongs do not necessarily have to be evil acts such as stealing or lying. As a recovering alcoholic, I can be in the wrong simply by the way I react to people or situations. If somebody injures me, for example, I am in the wrong by becoming indignant or vindictive about it. "It is a spiritual axiom that every time we are disturbed, no matter what the cause, there is something wrong to accept. We alcoholics can't afford this kind of thinking, even when we're innocent victims.

That statement is hard to accept, but it's good information for the alcoholic. There are times when we draw injury to ourselves by our own greed or carelessness. But there are other times when we're the victims of gratuitous treachery or cruelty. And we're not the only ones. All over the world, people are brooding deeply over injustices and wrongs they're not willing to accept. We alcoholics can't afford this kind of thinking, even when we're innocent victims.

Something we must avoid, at all costs, is the justified resentment. In dismissing the resentment, we are not saying that other people always do the right thing or that no harm occurs. We are only refusing to cause further harm to ourselves and others by becoming angry or disturbed. The sooner I can release my anger and resentment about an injury, the sooner I regain my own serenity and self-control. This also is true in cases where I have been injured but can seek legal advice or other remedies. In every case, I must eliminate all resentment or any desire for revenge or "getting even."

In the same spirit, I also learned that personal inventory helps in handling unexpected disagreements or misunderstandings with other people. There was a time when I blew up at auto mechanics who did not fix my car properly, when I wrote angry political letters, and when I berated the waiter if the food was cold. I might have thought I was being assertive, but I came to see that this behavior was immature and ineffective. It showed an unwillingness to trust other people, a fear that they would take advantage of me unless they were intimidated and brow-beaten. I couldn't have been more wrong.

Find Another Reason

Because I had so much difficulty with it—and so much relief when I finally took it—I consider Step Five one of the most useful tools in the A.A. Program. The essential idea of this Step is discussing one's shortcomings with another person. The same practice is implied in the Tenth Step, and there are times when we all need another person in order to take a good inventory. If something disturbs me, I need to find another person to talk it over with. And I've never done that without getting a changed feeling about the problem. There are times, too, when a problem can be discussed at an A.A. meeting, although it's often more satisfactory to take matters up with one person at a time.

Benefits

Good continued personal inventory—the Tenth Step—brings its own rewards. The most important benefit of this Step is that it strengthens and protects one's sobriety. It also brings rewards in several other areas:

Personal relationships. When I was drinking, there were a number of people I never spoke to as a result of long-standing disagreements. Sometimes I had forgotten the cause of the difficulty, but it did not matter. I was more interested in expressing my hatred than in patching things up. Today, however, I simply do not have these troubled relationships in my life. The practice of taking inventory and admitting my wrongs usually dissolves these misunderstandings in the initial stages.

Freedom from the fear of "being found out." I'm convinced that the refusal to face and to admit wrongs is rooted in feelings of inferiority and inadequacy. I tended to believe that I would be weakened and discredited if people knew me as I really was. There was a corresponding belief that if I could appear faultless on the outside, then I really would be without fault!

All this was wrong, and it showed that my own estimate of myself was based on appearing right in the view of other people. It was a great relief to embrace the honesty of A.A. and learn that I didn't have to maintain a facade any longer. By not pretending any longer to be a person I am not, I don't have to fear being "exposed" or "found out".

Freedom from guilt. One of the prices I paid for refusing to admit personal wrong was guilt. I was forced to continue denying guilt and to develop arguments to prove I had been right. This did not work, because the guilt always returned.

Ability to help others. One surprising benefit of admitting one's wrongs is becoming able to help others make similar admissions. It is something of a paradox: when I admit my own wrongs and stop accusing others, the way is shown to a real understanding of another's problems and what that person can do about it. Perhaps this is not hard to understand. We human beings have a natural resistance to self-righteous sermons and we feel belittled and "put down" when others point out our shortcomings. But, if someone practices self-honesty, we can sense this and will seek out that person for help with our problems.

Delay Can Be Costly

One final thought about the Tenth Step is to pay special attention to the word "promptly." The sooner I admit my wrong, the less harm it will do to me and to others. I still don't like to admit that I'm wrong, even in the little things. When I'm lost on the highway for example, I hate to check the road map or to stop for directions. This sometimes causes me to drive miles out of the way, sometimes on impossible roads. This same trait causes trouble in other ways.

On inventory matters, delay in admitting my wrong suggests that I'm secretly fighting the Tenth Step, hoping that the error will correct itself without any embarrassment or pain to me. But delay usually means that matters become worse. We can even "pay interest" in emotional pain when we delay in admitting that we're wrong.

But, however well we're doing with *the program*, none of us ever has it made. Eternal vigilance in taking a Tenth Step inventory is the price of freedom. The rewards in sobriety and personal growth are well worth the price.

STEP ELEVEN:
Maintaining the New Way of Life

Sought through prayer and meditation to improve our conscious contact with God *as we understood Him*, praying only for knowledge of His will for us and the power to carry that out.

MEL B.

Before finding sobriety in Alcoholics Anonymous, I displayed great faith and remarkable persistence—in drinking. I worshipped the bottle, I took every problem to the bottle, I leaned on the bottle with almost childlike trust. I persisted in this sick devotion long after the bottle god had repeatedly betrayed me and had wrecked my life.

After finding A.A., I still needed faith and persistence—but with a new direction. I looked to a Higher Power for the answers I had vainly sought in the bottle. This quest took faith, it took persistence, it took a strong determination to succeed in sobriety. But the Higher Power I found in A.A. has been a reliable guide and partner, never once betraying me and, in the meantime, repairing the wreckage of the past and providing a new way of life. Through the guidance of the Twelve-Step Program, I have been able to maintain and thoroughly enjoy this new way of life. What follows is my interpretation of Step Eleven of the Twelve Steps of Alcoholics Anonymous.

It is not always easy to maintain this new way of life. One of the dangers every recovering alcoholic faces is that boredom and disillusionment may set in after an early surge of inspiration and excitement. But the A.A. Program is structured to help us face these dangers. There is, for example, Step Eleven to remind us of the need to maintain the wonderful way of life we've been given.

Step Eleven is no quick fix. It is really Steps Two and Three practiced on a daily basis. Step Eleven can be our guide for the rest of our lives. Indeed, if Step Eleven is properly understood and carefully followed, some of the changes in our lives will border on the miraculous. We can have continuous sobriety, along with growth in the qualities we were seeking in the bottle but never found.

Step Eleven does exact a price, however, and we must pay it if we expect favorable results. There is a price in giving up the self-will that led us into trouble. Part of the price is working to become open-minded and willing about our need to change. Finally, Step Eleven calls for faith and persistence—the very qualities that we applied so wrongly to drinking!

Premise, Plan, and Purpose

The basic premise of Step Eleven should have been learned already and, it is hoped, accepted in the working of Steps Two and Three. This premise, which we learn from the A.A. literature and what others tell us, is that we can find a Higher Power who will be a personal source of both *guidance* and *power*. This Higher Power can be God or whatever else we choose to believe it to be. A.A. does not directly tell us what to believe about the nature of our Higher Power. *The program* implies, however, that our Higher Power is a loving Power who has only the best interests of each individual in mind. A definition of our Higher Power is even suggested in the Second Tradition of A.A.: "A loving God as He may express Himself in our group conscience."[1]

The basic *premise* of A.A. also includes the idea that this loving Power wants to enrich our lives. All of us want the abundant life, and we had deluded ourselves into thinking that alcohol or drugs would give that blessed state to us. It is exciting to realize that we truly can have an abundant life if we accept the protection and care of our Higher Power. The A.A. pioneers, even when they were a small group of about a hundred recovering alcoholics, believed that this abundant life could be had for the asking. "We found that God does not make too hard terms with those who seek Him," they wrote. "To us, the Realm of Spirit is broad, roomy, all-inclusive, never exclusive or forbidding to those who earnestly seek. It is open, we believe, to all people."[2]

Step Eleven also includes a search *plan* for those who wish to enter this Realm of Spirit. The search for a Higher Power takes place in our own thinking. "Sought through prayer and meditation" deals solely with our own personal methods of communicating with our Higher Power. This is an individual matter, and what works best for one person might be irritating to another. What counts is not the style or manner of the prayer but the effects produced in our lives.

Early A.A. members in Akron and New York had group prayer on their knees, a practice abandoned by the Fellowship in the early 1940s. It is not necessary that we pray on our knees, unless as individuals we feel it makes the prayer more effective. Nor is it necessary to pray in the company of others, unless one prefers to do so. This does not mean that it is wrong to pray with others, but we should not pray only for appearances. Some of us benefit from church services and other forms of group prayer.

Purpose also is included in Step Eleven, in whatever form of prayer and meditation we choose to follow. The purpose of prayer and meditation is only to improve one's *conscious contact* with God as one understands Him. How can we tell if we're getting anywhere with our prayers and meditations? There should be signs along the way to tell us if we're on the right path. One sign is a deep sense of gratitude, accompanied by a feeling of belonging in the world at last. We should also have growth in self-esteem and perhaps a feeling that we have rights and are becoming worthy. We may have a sense of being guided and sustained as we go about our affairs. We may even experience an occasional sense of joy about sobriety and work.

The Mystery of Guidance

However, there are dangers and difficulties in the prayer and meditation program. Our minds are somewhat like early radio receiving sets, which picked up static and conflicting messages. We ought to seek guidance, and we are often told to do so by our sponsors and other A.A. members. Yet, "seeking guidance" can be a very tricky matter and for very understandable reasons.

Bill W., the A.A. cofounder who wrote most of the A.A. Program materials, had this problem much in mind when he warned that the person who tries to run his or her life rigidly, with self-serving demands of God for replies, is a particularly disconcerting person. Bill wrote about such a person, "To any questioning or criticism of his actions he instantly proffers his reliance upon prayer for guidance in all matters great or small. He may have forgotten the possibility that his own wishful thinking and the human tendency to rationalize have distorted his so-called guidance. With the best of intentions, he tends to force his own will into all sorts of situations and problems with the comfortable assurance that he is acting under God's specific direction. Under such an illusion, he can, of course, create great havoc without in the least intending it."[3]

In Step Eleven, guidance also is defined as "knowledge of God's will for us and the power to carry that out." This means that we do not seek guidance for other persons, although our guidance may include service to others.

But how are we to know the will of our Higher Power? Here again, the messages can be faulty and difficult to understand, like the stuff coming over those early receiving sets. Our own desires and opinions are so much a part of us that we are likely to view the will of a Higher Power in terms of our own feelings.

Superstition and early religious training also can play a part in this. One of my friends, years ago, suffered greatly because he did not believe God would ever forgive him for his years of drinking. This belief was harmful, because he did not think that he could please God or that he was worthy of God's help. I have known others who believe that God wants them to suffer or to fail in something, and these beliefs tend to be self-fulfilling.

When my confusion on this subject becomes too thick, I've found comfort in the ancient parable of the prodigal son, which was almost custom-designed for the recovering alcoholic. In this parable, the father represents God, who runs to meet the son even though the latter has squandered his inheritance in selfish, sinful behavior. The son is so beaten that he has decided not to ask his father for anything, and yet the father gives him a ring, beautiful clothing, and has a celebration because the son has returned!

But there also is an elder brother in this parable, a person who always did his duty and never left his father. He is extremely displeased about the favorable treatment of his younger brother, and he refuses to take part in the celebration.

The lesson I get from this parable is that God seeks us even more than we seek Him. However, there are two parts of our nature that are in conflict: we are both the younger brother and the elder brother. God wants to give us everything, wants complete union with us, and for no other reason than that we are His children. But there is a stern Elder Brother within us that holds back, that tells us we have to earn everything, that only righteous and deserving people are entitled to union with God.

However, the younger-brother side of our nature (the rebellious, self-centered side) also has to make a concession to make contact with our Higher Power. This concession is the complete willingness to accept God's will and whatever terms are offered. In the parable, for example, the prodigal son was so defeated that he was even willing to be a servant in his father's house. Although his father surprised him with love and gifts, none of these benefits were obtained by demanding them or by pleading and begging. Many of us who come to A.A. have the same experience. We are no longer in a position to demand anything, and the best we can hope for is relief from the terrible agony of alcoholism or other drug dependency. But we often have been surprised by unexpected improvements in other areas of our lives.

Step Eleven keeps this idea before us—we don't *demand* anything from our Higher Power, but we let it work out in a natural way. The best method of meeting our needs will always be chosen if we leave matters to God. This, of course, is not the way we like to work. We are tempted to issue orders, to pray things like: "I want *this* job!" or, "I want *this* person to marry me!" or, "I want *this* problem cleared up in *this* manner by next Tuesday!"

In fact, however, we do not have to tell our Higher Power what we need or what will be best for us. The Greek philosopher Pythagoras expressed a similar thought, "Do not pray for yourself: you do not know what will help you." This simply means that we cannot see the Big Picture, only a part of it. We often cannot perceive the long-term effects of something that seems attractive and reasonable at the moment. But if we pray and meditate in the right way, some of these things will be made clear to us.

One A.A. member, for example, became quite disappointed when he prayed for guidance about a business negotiation that fell through. Had he succeeded, however, he would not have been in a position to take advantage of an even better opportunity that appeared a few weeks later. Bill W., in 1935, had a harsh setback when he was defeated in a proxy fight for control of a small-machine tool company. His desperation drove him to get in touch with another alcoholic, however, who joined him in the founding of A.A. We never really know when defeats will become victories. There is also a saying, frequently heard in

A.A., that warns us to be careful what we pray for, because we might get it! The point of this saying is that the thing we want today could very well prove to be exactly what we don't want six months from now.

A Harmony of Wills

Still, it is also a mistake to believe that what we want is always wrong or that our own will always is necessarily in opposition to the will of our Higher Power. More than likely, our common failure is not that our aims are wrong; it is in not seeking the *highest* and *best* that is possible for us. It is also true that God's will for us must exist in our natural talents and abilities, and also in the circumstances of our lives. We can take ourselves as we are at this point and seek to merge our own aims and purposes with God's plan.

As recovering alcoholics, we can make several reasonable assumptions about God's will in our lives. One, God wants us to stay sober and also to help others. We get this feeling strongly at many A.A. meetings or when we reflect on what has happened in our lives. We can also look upon the A.A. Fellowship as a channel of God's grace, although it is certainly not the only one and perhaps not the best one. But, it is probably the best one for alcoholics.

Another assumption is that God's will means carrying out reasonable duties and responsibilities. Alcohol or drugs cause us to neglect our families and to ignore other responsibilities, but our spiritual program should give us the maturity and strength to do the right things in life. We should not neglect our jobs or our families, and we also should feel certain responsibilities toward society—responsibilities that are probably within God's plan.

Finally, it's also a reasonable assumption that we each have a "place," a part to play, in life. One young woman said at an A.A. meeting, "God could not have made a Stradivarius violin without Stradivarius," and that is entirely true. And each of us has things that only we can do and a place that only we can fill. Some of the good work we could do—particularly in A.A.— might not ever be done unless we do it.

Whatever we learn about our Higher Power's will for us, we also should not forget that the power or means is always provided to carry it out—that is implicitly stated in Step Eleven. We cannot always say how this works for every person or in every case. In some ways, it may be similar to getting a business assignment from an employer. If the company expects you to make a business trip, they will usually provide expense money, credit cards, introductions, and other necessities. God seems to work in the same way. The early A.A. members, even in the midst of the Depression, always got by and found the means to carry out their work.

We also have work to do for a Higher Employer who wants to provide for us. This is important work, and it requires a merging of our wills and God's will. Like the father of the prodigal son, God needs us just as much as we need God. But we also have to accept the *plan* and *purpose*. Without a Higher Power, we cannot do the things we really need to do.

STEP TWELVE:
Language of the Heart

Having had a spiritual awakening as the result of these steps, we tried to carry this message to alcoholics and to practice these principles in all our affairs.

PETER CONVERSE McDONALD

> Because of our kinship in suffering, and because our common means of deliverance are effective only when constantly carried to others, our channels of contact have always been charged with the Language of the Heart.—Bill W.

What follows is a guide to each of the three topics in Step Twelve. In the first section, we will look at what it means to have a "spiritual awakening as a result of these Steps." How does it happen? How do we know a spiritual awakening is taking place? What's it like to awaken spiritually?

In the second section, we will consider different ways of "carrying this message." How do we go about making a Twelfth-Step call? Are there different kinds? What "message" are we carrying? When can we start doing Twelfth-Step work? Do we have to wait until we've made at least a start on the other eleven Steps?

In the final section, we will focus on using the Twelve Steps "in all our affairs," not just applying them to our disease. How can these Steps be used in our relationships, on the job, at home? Again, Step Twelve is taking us beyond ourselves and our chemical dependency to other people and situations. We may be surprised to find how helpful the Twelve Steps are when applied to "all our affairs." In a very real way, they become a way of life. Applied to all areas of our lives, the Twelve Steps can bring us to a joy of living.

"Having Had a Spiritual Awakening as the Result of These Steps"

Just exactly what is a spiritual awakening, and how do we know when we are waking up spiritually?

The opening words of Step Twelve imply that a spiritual awakening is something that has occurred in the past and is now completed. But it's important to realize that such an awakening is an ongoing, never-ending *process*. It may have begun sometime in the past when we took the First Step, but it continues for the rest of our lives. It is not a distinct event with a clear beginning and ending. That is the first thing to remember about spiritual awakenings.

The second is that every person's spiritual awakening is unique, that no two are exactly alike. But that doesn't mean that each is not just as real and valid. However, spiritual awakenings have some common denominators. They often follow long periods of mental or emotional darkness. We may have felt terribly alone, as if no one understood us.

Spiritual awakenings are often described as just that— awakenings. They represent a coming to conscious awareness of ourselves as we really are, an awareness of a Power greater than ourselves, which may be outside ourselves, or deep within ourselves, or both. Where there was darkness, now there is light. We can see things more realistically. Indeed we can see things we never saw before. Most people experience a sense of letting go. But in addition, many of us, especially women, report a gaining of power, a coming to our true selves after surrendering. There is a sense of grounding of ourselves in a power we didn't know before.

I like to think of spiritual awakening in terms of waking up in the morning. The process seems to start before we are conscious and awake. We may start to toss and turn in our sleep. We may dream. We may become uncomfortable, stiff, too hot, or too cold. We sometimes open one eye and check to see what the weather is, then groan and fall back asleep for a few minutes. But we're starting to wake up.

Then the alarm goes off, and we're at least somewhat awake. We know we are conscious. We can see the room around us and ourselves sitting sleepily on the edge of the bed.

The beginning of recovery is like that—the beginning of our spiritual awakening. We toss and turn, become very uncomfortable, perhaps very ill or very separated from our families and friends in some way. We groan, turn over, and go back to sleep, denying that there is anything wrong with us, not yet willing to face the reality of ourselves and our condition. We put our head under the pillow, trying to keep out the light of day that will make it clear to us that we have a problem, that we're powerless over alcohol or other drugs and that our lives are unmanageable. We fight to stay asleep spiritually.

But the alarm has, indeed, gone off. Perhaps some crisis forces us to wake up, to see ourselves as we really are. There may be an intervention by our families or employers. Or in a rare moment of insight, we may realize that we have a problem and need help. But one way or another, when the alarm goes off, we admit we are powerless. Our spiritual awakening has begun.

Once we are awake, how do we know the process is continuing? What are some of the signs that tell us we're making spiritual progress?

Probably the most practical way to tell is to look at our behavior. Is it any different than it was in the past, before we began waking up? To continue the metaphor of getting up in the morning, are we now getting out of bed right away, rather than hitting the snooze alarm for a few more minutes of sleep? Are we eager for the day ahead? If so, that's a sign of spiritual progress.

Other examples of changing behavior: do we procrastinate

less? Are we getting things done more quickly? Do we admit our mistakes more readily, both to ourselves and to others? Can we even laugh about them a little bit? Are we asking for help when we need it, rather than being stubborn and thinking we don't need help? Are we more open and honest about our shortcomings? Do we accept them as part of who we are? Are we beginning to claim the good parts of ourselves? Are we more willing to let go of our resentments toward others? Do we make amends when we hurt someone else, sincerely admitting we were wrong? On a daily basis, are we more aware of our behavior and attitudes? Do we find ourselves taking time each day to be quiet, perhaps to meditate or to pray? Are we reaching out to help others who may need us?

If the answer to any one of those questions is yes, then we can say that we are waking up spiritually and that our spiritual awakening continues.

No doubt you've noticed that the foregoing is a review of some of the Twelve Steps from a behavioral point of view. The point is that if we are working the Steps, using them in our daily lives to stay sober or chemically free, then we are certainly making spiritual progress. And it's important to remember that we don't have to be working all of the Steps every day in order to be making progress. One is enough for starters. But as our awakening continues, we'll probably find that we're using more and more of the Steps on a daily basis.

The behavior of others may also indicate to us that we are making progress on a spiritual level. Are our spouse and children more trusting of us? Have we regained some respect from them or from fellow employees and friends? Are we given more responsibility at work or at home? If so, it's probably because those around us see some positive changes in us. They may see spiritual progress that we haven't noticed until they illuminate it by their new trust and respect.

However, my own experience as a recovering person reminds me that the regaining of trust and responsibility and respect, especially from our spouse, may happen very slowly. After all I was a pretty sick person for a long time, and I had to prove—by my own behavior—that I could be trusted by my wife. She put up with my drinking and bizarre behavior for years, and it has taken years for her to trust me again. So I had to be patient with her, as patient as she was with me. The point is that we need not be hurt or disappointed if we don't immediately receive the respect and trust we want.

What are some other ways of knowing that we're awakening spiritually? One is that we may have experiences that can be called spiritual.

A spiritual *experience* is very different from the ongoing spiritual *awakening*. It is an event that has a distinct beginning and end. That's a crucial distinction. Some of us used to think that if we had such an experience, we were "converted" or "born again," or that suddenly we "got it" and were "healed." We thought that was all there was to it. That's not the case. Spiritual experiences are merely signs along the way that we're making progress in our spiritual awakening.

Spiritual experiences come in many different forms, and not everyone has them. Although rare, some are very dramatic. Most seem to be subtle. Spiritual experiences can be, and usually are, common everyday events that in our new sobriety we now see as having a spiritual element to them. And like spiritual awakenings, spiritual experiences also can be unique to the person.

What are some examples of spiritual experiences that will tell us we're making progress? The dramatic type is the one that comes to mind first. Sometimes it can happen right at the beginning of our spiritual awakening, although that's rare. One person I know said he suddenly had a visual replay of all his drinking life and behavior—in the course of just a few seconds—and realized he was alcoholic. He then went and got help. He called it "enlightenment," and for him it was not only a spiritual experience, but a mystical one as well.

Probably the rest of us may have to be content with less amazing circumstances. My own spiritual experiences usually take me by surprise. They're ordinary events like watching the sun go down over a lake, seeing a smile on a baby's face, listening to good music, and the like.

Spiritual experiences can also be moments of insight when we say to ourselves, "Aha! Of course. I'd never made that connection before, but I see it clearly now." You know the feeling—when something suddenly falls into place for you and is obvious to you. That's a spiritual experience—for me, anyway. Others may choose to interpret it differently.

Such experiences are not always positive ones at the time. In fact, sometimes they can be very painful. It's only in retrospect that one can look at them as being spiritual in nature.

For instance, I once had to end a relationship with a woman I loved very much. Both of us had invested a great deal of ourselves in the relationship, and both of us had tried very hard to make it work. But after a time it became clear that we were not compatible people, and so we mutually agreed to part.

The last time I saw her was excruciatingly painful. We finally had nothing left to say to each other, and so we hugged and said goodbye. I knew she was crying as she turned away to go, and I wondered why I wasn't. I just felt numb, empty. A little later, I went to a place that is very special to me—to be alone, to cry, to do whatever I had to do. I found myself talking to my Higher Power, asking why this had to happen, why all my hopes and dreams and plans had been destroyed. In fact, I got very angry with my Higher Power. I did a lot of yelling and swearing. I also got angry at the woman for not being the person I wanted her to be. Finally, I got angry at myself because I couldn't make the relationship work. I was powerless. Then I cried not just a few sniffles, but huge racking sobs that seemed to come from the deepest part of me.

Afterward I felt empty again. But something was different. Some of the heaviness was gone. There was some peace, some acceptance of the fact that the relationship was ended, perhaps even some serenity.

Even though it was terribly painful, that hour or so was a spiritual experience for me. Why? Because I was very aware of my God's presence within me, because I was very aware of myself and how much I was hurting, and how much my friend apparently had been hurting.

I think that is a common denominator to all spiritual experiences, no matter how large or small the experiences may be. In all of them there is some awareness of Another, of a Higher Power, a Greater Good, a Deeper Self, a God Within or Without. However it is for you, such an awareness is found in every spiritual experience.

And that's what tells us we are making progress spiritually, that our spiritual awakening is continuing. It's the fact that every once in a while, we are aware of some other Power operating in our lives, sometimes in us or in other people, sometimes in nature, and sometimes in common everyday occurrences.

"We Tried to Carry this Message to Alcoholics"

Here is the heart of the Twelfth Step. This is what it's really all about. "Carrying the message" means that we reach out to other alcoholics or chemically dependent people and tell them the story of our own spiritual awakening. The message we carry is that as a result of the Steps, we came to awaken spiritually, began to recover, and continue to do so. It is a message of hope.

We take the Twelfth Step for two reasons. The first and primary one is to strengthen our own recovery, to continue our own spiritual growth by sharing ourselves with another human being. Something happens to us when we do that. There is value in giving of ourselves. We always receive something back, whether it's new strength or new self-insight, the satisfaction of attempting to help another person, or the realization that someone else needs us, that we have something of value to share. That something of value is ourselves.

The second reason for taking the Twelfth Step is that by doing so others may come to awaken spiritually. In our story, they may see some hope for themselves, for they may identify with part of our story. Perhaps the circumstances of our drinking or using may be similar to theirs. They may say to themselves, "Well, if that person can do it, can stop using or drinking, then just maybe so can I."

Step Twelve is called "the language of the heart" because that's exactly what it is. When we take the Twelfth Step and talk with someone else, we are talking from our hearts. We're being as honest and as open as we can about who we are, where we've been, and how we got to where we are today in our recovery and spiritual growth.

Those of us who are recovering have found many different methods of taking the Twelfth Step. But in every method, we share at least a part of ourselves—whether it's by telling some or all of our story, by giving our time or energy to help someone else, or by serving others in some way.

When can we start to take the Twelfth Step? Are there any special qualifications we need, any special training? To answer the first question, if we have taken Step One, if we've been through treatment, or if we've been to a meeting, then we've already done Twelfth-Step work. As to the second question, the only qualification necessary is the ability to tell our stories as honestly as we can. No special training is needed. Being ourselves is enough.

Just by our presence at a meeting, without saying a word, we are helping the other people at the meeting by sharing ourselves. Being there is a way to share ourselves, perhaps even the best way. And when we do speak, even if it's only to smile and say hello to a newcomer at the meeting, we are working the Twelfth Step. It's as simple as that.

Traditionally, Twelfth-Step work has been done by visiting with another individual who is perceived as needing help, to help him or her awaken spiritually and begin the process of recovery. That individual usually is still drinking or using and can't see the reality of his or her behavior and its effects on other people. Such visits can be at the request of the alcoholic or the family. The visit is made because we see a problem with a friend or relative, and we want to help if we can. These visits are generally known as Twelfth-Step "calls."

In addition, there are many other ways of doing Twelfth-Step work as part of our program of recovery. Doing volunteer work at a treatment center is one method. Volunteering to spend time answering phones at A.A. Central Service is another. Visiting with patients in a detox clinic or with residents in a halfway house are two more. And some recovering alcoholics and chemically dependent people leave their names and phone numbers with A.A. Central Service in their city, so if someone calls and wants help, A.A. will have helpers available.

Some of us who are recovering also may be asked to participate in an "intervention." That, too, is a form of Twelfth-Step work. In those cases we usually know the person well, and vice versa, either because we are a member of the family, a close friend, or a fellow employee. Interventions are generally carried out with the help or advice of a professionally trained counselor. They serve to confront a person with the reality of his or her drinking or using behavior, after which the person is usually asked to make a choice as to what he or she wishes to do. Usually the choice is clear, but sometimes it is painful. Either the person seeks help in some way (through treatment or going to A.A., for instance), or he or she will lose his or her job, or the spouse will ask for a separation. Whatever the situation or circumstance, in all Twelfth-Step work we share ourselves by telling our story: how we came to be dependent, what it was like for us, how we came to be sober or chemically free, and how our spiritual awakening took place.

In Twelfth-Step work it's often appropriate to make observations about the behavior of the person we are trying to help. In such cases, it's important to report only the facts of the behavior that we have observed and to do so in a caring and nonjudgmental way. That way, the person we are trying to help will not be put on the defensive.

However, usually all we have to do is tell our story. By so doing we are holding up a mirror to others as if to say, "Look, this is what happened to me. Do you see any of yourself in here, in my story?" That is another way of presenting the reality of their own drinking or using behavior in a manner they may be able to accept. It is less confrontational and less threatening than directly pointing out their own behavior. It is a way of saying to them that it's okay to be the way I was and the way they are now.

Through painful trial and error, those of us who have done Twelfth-Step work have developed a set of guidelines or suggestions. Those guidelines help us to be more effective in transmitting the message and encouraging the recipient to ask for our help. What follows are not hard and fast rules, but I know they help make Twelfth-Step work more effective and less frustrating for those of us who make Twelfth-Step calls.

Make Twelfth-Step calls with another person. Don't try to do one by yourself. One reason is the person you're visiting with will then have double the chance of identifying with one of the two stories he or she is hearing. Another, more practical reason for taking someone with you is for self-protection. The person on whom you are calling may be drunk and may become violent. By the time you get there, he or she may have passed out. If the person agrees to get help and you need to provide transportation, it's a good idea to have someone in the car with you. Have your partner sit in the back seat with the person you are helping.

If you are calling on a person of the opposite sex, take someone of that same sex with you. If you're a man calling on a woman, she has a ready-made excuse for not identifying with you because you're not a woman. But if you have a woman with you, she won't have that excuse. Indeed, she may be able to see some of herself in your partner's story.

Tell your own story. Stick to it and be as honest and specific as you can. Talk about what your behavior was like when you were drinking or using, what you did and what you said. Tell how much you drank or used and how it affected you. Tell how you felt about yourself when you were drinking or using. Tell how it affected your family, your job. The more you say, the better the person will be able to identify with at least part of your story.

Then talk about your own recovery. Tell how it started. Tell when and how you started to awaken spiritually, although you need not use that phrase, especially if you know the person would have a problem with it. Talk about what finally made you admit that you were powerless and that your life was indeed unmanageable. If you went to treatment, talk about what it was like. If someone took you to a meeting, tell what that was like. Talk about what your life has been like since. Be honest about that, too. For instance, my own life hasn't been all peaches and cream since I took the First Step, but it's much better than it was when I was drinking.

Offer help because you care and you want to, not just because you think the person needs it (even if it's obvious to you that he or she does). The person may even ask your advice on what to do. In that case, try to act as a facilitator in the decision making. You can do that by listing the various options you know and by making a recommendation.

Have no expectations. The person may decide to continue drinking or using. In fact, that is usually the case. It's important to know that so we aren't disappointed or upset because the person has not responded to our story and offer of help. We can take solace in the fact that we did our best. We planted a seed of thought. The person we visited knows where to get help. We also know that we have succeeded in a big way because we have taken the Twelfth Step as part of our own program of recovery.

We have done something for ourselves that is helping us to stay sober or chemically free.

If the person does accept our help, be prepared to follow through. That may mean taking him or her to a meeting, arranging for admission to a treatment center or outpatient program, or even providing transportation to a treatment center. If treatment is the decision, stay in touch by phone or letter. Let the person know you care and are standing by. When treatment concludes, offer to take him or her to meetings. We know what it was like at the beginning of recovery and how much we appreciated people who cared about us.

Perhaps more important than anything else, always show both care and respect for the person you are calling on. Being judgmental won't do any good, and as recovering people ourselves, we have no right to be judgmental. We know about denial, for instance. And we know the person we are visiting is deserving of our concern and respect simply because he or she is a human being, like us, and one who may be very ill. So it's important not to let the other person sense any impatience or anger or judgment in us. Such feelings are entirely out of place in a Twelfth-Step visit—and they are certainly no good for our own recovery process. In fact, they are signs that we still have work to do on ourselves. But if we have enough respect for the person to let him or her be, and if we can remember that we can only change ourselves and no one else (I've often said the Serenity Prayer silently while on a Twelfth-Step call), we will make it much easier for that person to request and accept our help.

These are just a few general suggestions that can be applied to any kind of Twelfth-Step work. As you gain experience, you will discover what works and what doesn't for you, and you'll develop your own guidelines.

"And to Practice These Principles in All Our Affairs"

"These principles" mean the Twelve Steps. "Affairs" mean all aspects of our daily lives.

Until now, we have been concerned primarily with getting sober or straight. We've been using the Twelve Steps to do that. We've admitted that we are powerless over alcohol or drugs and that our lives had become unmanageable because of our drinking or using. But as we gain some sobriety, we begin to realize that it isn't just alcohol or drugs over which we're powerless; we're powerless over many other things as well. We begin to see we are powerless over our spouse, children, friends, and colleagues at work. We begin to see that we have no control over their behavior or thoughts or attitudes or feelings. We can't make them do or say or feel what we want. If we try, we know our lives will become unmanageable again.

Of course, it would be wonderful if our wife or husband loved and trusted us as perhaps they once did. But we can't make them do so. We have no control over their feelings. So what do we do? We believe that a Power greater than ourselves will restore us to sanity, and we turn the problem over to that Power. We let go, using Step Three.

Perhaps our supervisor at work isn't giving us the raise we want or more responsibility in our job. We could choose to get angry and resentful or to feel sorry for ourselves. But would that do any good? The alternative is to turn over our resentment or self-pity (Step Seven) and get on with our job. Perhaps if we work hard enough, we will gain the supervisor's respect, and then we'll get that raise or increased responsibility. Perhaps not. But by going back to Step One, we realize we are powerless over our supervisor and his or her attitude toward us. All we can change is ourselves. In the end, we may have to consider a different job where we might get the respect we feel we deserve.

In the course of our Fourth and Fifth Steps, we may have discovered that one of our character defects is impatience (certainly, it's one of mine). In our daily lives, what can we do about it? If our husband or wife is continually late, do we still get impatient or are we beginning to learn how to let go and let him or her be late? Can we find something constructive to do instead of just waiting impatiently? If so, we're practicing the Steps in another aspect of our daily lives.

In this case, Step One helps us realize we are powerless over our spouse's actions. In Step Three we turn it over, in Step Four we identify our impatience, and in Step Seven we let go of the impatience. In Step Nine we tell our spouse we've been impatient with him or her and apologize, making amends. In Step Ten we continue to monitor our behavior and attitudes on a daily basis to see if we're becoming more patient. In Step Eleven we may pray or meditate on what our Higher Power wills for us in regard to our spouse, his or her lateness, and our impatience. And in Step Twelve, we may find a way to help our spouse be on time, perhaps by sharing how we used to be late all the time and how we came to be on time. Perhaps then our spouse may change his or her behavior. Or we can change our own behavior, quit waiting, and let our latecomer eat alone.

That may be an overly simplistic example of how the Twelve Steps can be applied in an everyday situation of our lives, but it illustrates how it can be done. And when it is, it makes life much easier to live.

If we use the Twelve Steps in all our affairs, as the Twelfth Step suggests, we will find ourselves truly changed people. We will find new serenity. We will be selfless people, honestly caring about our families and friends. We will be more understanding, less critical, more giving of ourselves. And we will receive the love and care and trust and respect that we know we deserve when we are living our lives to the best of our abilities.

Obviously, it is asking too much of ourselves to demand that we practice all the Steps all the time. I know I don't. But we can make a start. We can want to do the best we can.

As I go about my Twelfth-Step work, carrying the message and practicing the Twelve Steps as best I can in all my affairs, I often think of the prayer attributed to St. Francis of Assisi. While this prayer is helpful in previous Steps, I've adopted it as my Twelfth-Step prayer so it bears repeating here:

Lord make me an instrument of your peace
  Where there is hatred, let me sow love
  Where there is injury, pardon
  Where there is doubt, faith
  Where there is despair, hope
  Where there is darkness, light
  Where there is sadness, joy.

O Divine Master, grant that I may not so much seek
  To be consoled, as to console
  To be understood, as to understand
  To be loved, as to love.

For
  It is in giving that we receive
  It is in pardoning that we are pardoned
  It is in dying that we are born to eternal life.

Notes

Step Two

1. *Alcoholics Anonymous* (New York: A.A. World Services, 1976) is often called the Big Book.

Step Five

1. *Twelve Steps and Twelve Traditions* (New York: A.A. World Services, 1953).

Step Nine

1. John Powell, S.J., *A Reason to Live, A Reason to Die* (Allen, Tex.: Argus, 1975), 126–127.

2. *Alcoholics Anonymous*, 82.

3. God grant me the serenity
   To accept the things I cannot change,
   The courage to change the things I can,
   And the wisdom to know the difference.

Step Ten

1. *Alcoholics Anonymous*, 64.

2. *Alcoholics Anonymous*, 84.

3. James Allen, *As a Man Thinketh* (Old Tappan, N.J.: Revell, 1905), 9.

4. *Twelve Steps and Twelve Traditions*, 92.

Step Eleven

1. *Twelve Steps and Twelve Traditions*, 132.

2. *Alcoholics Anonymous*, 46.

3. *Twelve Steps and Twelve Traditions*, 106.

Other Readings

Alcoholics Anonymous. 3d ed. New York: A.A. World Services, 1976.

Christ, Carol P. *Diving Deep and Surfacing: Women Writers on Spiritual Quest*. Boston: Beacon, 1980.

Clinebell, Howard J., Jr. *Understanding and Counseling the Alcoholic*. Nashville, Tenn.: Abingdon, 1968.

Kurtz, Ernest. *Not-God: A History of Alcoholics Anonymous*. Center City, Minn.: Hazelden Educational Materials, 1979.

Twelve Steps and Twelve Traditions. New York: A.A. World Services, 1953.

Wilson, William G. *As Bill Sees It*. New York: A.A. World Services, 1967.

The Authors

Introduction: Karen Elliott, Director of Hazelden Educational Materials, is also the anonymous author of *Each Day a New Beginning* and, under the name Karen Casesy, is the author of *The Love Book* and the coauthor of the *The Promise of a New Day*.

Step One: William Springborn is program director of Hanley-Hazelden in West Palm Beach, Florida.

Steps Two and Three: James G. Jensen is the former program director of the Chemical Dependency Rehabilitation Center, St. Joseph's Hospital, St. Paul, Minnesota.

Step Four: The Hazelden Foundation

Step Five: Edward C. Sellner has a Ph.D. in Pastoral Theology from the University of Notre Dame. He has counseled chemically dependent people and their families in Indiana and Minnesota, worked with the Hazelden Continuing Education Department, and taught pastoral theology.

Steps Six and Seven: James Brandon, a chemical dependency family counselor, has contributed to the *American Handbook of Alcoholism*.

Steps Eight and Nine: Pat M. is a chemical dependency counselor in Minneapolis.

Steps Ten and Eleven: Mel B. is a recovering alcoholic.

Step Twelve: Peter Converse McDonald is a freelance writer who dedicates his essay to Priscilla, Alexa, Hadley, and Frank I., "all of whom are sharing their spiritual awakenings with me and allowing me to share mine with them."